RUNNING
HOT

RUNNING
HOT

LISA TAMATI

ALLEN&UNWIN

In memory of Andrea Needham.

With thanks to my family, friends and Gerhard.

First published 2009
This edition published in 2011

Allen & Unwin
Level 3
228 Queen Street
Auckland
New Zealand
Phone: (64 9) 377 3800
Fax: (64 9) 377 3811
Email: auckland@allenandunwin.com
Web: www.allenandunwin.com

National Library of New Zealand Cataloguing-in-Publication Data

Tamati, Lisa, 1971–
Running hot / Lisa Tamati and Nicola McCloy
ISBN 978-1-877505-09-6
1. Tamati, Lisa, 1971– 2. Long-distance runners—Biography.
I. McCloy, Nicola, 1971– II. Title.
796.42092—dc 22

ISBN 978 1 877505 09 6

Typeset in 8.5 pt Bitstream Carmina by Janet Hunt
Cover design by Katy Yiakmis
Cover image by Mike Scott

Printed in Australia by McPherson's Printing Group

10 9 8 7 6 5 4 3 2 1

CONTENTS

INTRODUCTION

Me and my big mouth! Why can't I just keep my mouth shut and be normal? It's 9.45 on the morning of 14 July 2008. I am freaking out badly but putting on a brave face. In fifteen minutes, the starter's gun will go off. Once I hear that gun, I know I won't be sleeping for a few days but that's the least of my worries. It will also mean the start of one of the hardest races on earth — the Badwater Ultramarathon. Why the hell did I ever tell anyone that I wanted to do this?

Yep, that's Badwater as in Badwater, Death Valley. It's the lowest part of the United States at 85 metres below sea level. It is also one of the hottest places in the world with temperatures recorded as high as 56.7°C. I just hope that Death Valley doesn't live up to its name over the next few days!

I'm standing at the start line and it's about 50°C. Ahead of me lies 217 kilometres of one of the most demanding and extreme running races in the world. From where I stand now, I've got to walk, run, dance and drag myself through places with welcoming names like Furnace Creek, Devil's Cornfield and Lone Pine. But that's not the worst of it, once I've made it through the desert, there's a couple of mountain passes to climb culminating with making my way up 2500 metres to the slopes of Mount Whitney, the highest point in the mainland United States.

It's a race I've wanted to tackle for about eight years but until now I haven't had the money or the experience. I've been ultra-running for thirteen years and I've covered more than 50,000 kilometres in races and training.

I've run in the Sahara, Libyan and Arabian deserts but I'm still not sure that will be enough to prepare me for what is to come. The heat here easily outdoes anything I've experienced before and here I am alongside some of my absolute heroes — Dean Karnazes and David Goggins. I'm completely star struck and can't believe that I'm lining up next to them. OK, so rookies like me would normally start in the 6 am bunch running through the valley in the coolest part of the day but I've got a film crew with me so I've been lined up to start at 10 am with the elite runners. I hope like hell I'm ready.

How am I going to do this? I've got 60 hours to cover those 217 gruelling kilometres. But I can't think of the days ahead in that way. I've got to focus on moving as little as possible, on reserving my energy, taking one step at a time then one kilometre at a time. I can't begin to think about the whole 217 kilometres ahead of me — that would just blow my mind.

It's just minutes to the start now. I've eaten and drunk so much to build my reserves that I feel bloated. I just want to get going. Chris Kostman, the race director, gives us all a wee pep talk. The American anthem plays and the countdown begins. Three . . . two . . . one. The gun goes off.

I've visualised this moment over and over again in the past couple of years. Now that I'm here, it's completely surreal. I can't quite believe that I'm really here. Me and my big bloody mouth!

GROWING UP IN TARANAKI

Be constantly in search of knowledge

When I was born, Mum and Dad lived in New Plymouth in a wee one bedroom house. Dad was working as a printer and Mum worked as a teacher. Not long after I came along, they built a house out in a rural area near Bell Block. Around that time, Dad decided he'd had enough of the printing industry and joined the Fire Service — it seems that a dislike of the nine-to-five life runs in the family.

I was two when my brother Dawson was born. Eighteen months after Dawson was born, Mitchell came along and rounded out our family. Life on the farmlet was pretty cool but always really busy. There were always chooks to feed and animals to look after.

One of the main things that shaped my childhood was that I had severe asthma from the age of about two. We lived about 15 kilometres out of town, we didn't have any neighbours and Dad was in the fire brigade working 24 hours on and 24 hours off, so it was pretty full on whenever I had a bad asthma attack. Mum would always have to arrange my auntie Peggy or grandmother to come and look after the boys before racing me into the hospital in New Plymouth. When we got there, I'd get put in a Ventolin tent until I came right. Mum was always right by my side the whole time. I believe that's why my relationship with my mum is as close as it is today.

I just remember the attacks being terrifying, I couldn't breathe and I didn't know why. Right throughout my childhood I had to fight with asthma to achieve what I wanted. I never really considered it as a disability; it was just something I had to work around.

The one thing that did stay with me because of the asthma was that I was really fearful of dying and I was a bit more dependent on Mum and Dad than a lot of other kids might be. I didn't like being away from home much because I was scared that if I stayed at someone else's house they wouldn't know what to do if I had an asthma attack. The only person I knew could deal with it apart from Mum and Dad was Nana so I was always happy going to her place.

Thankfully though, Mum and Dad didn't wrap me up in cotton wool because of the asthma. They decided the best way for it to be treated was learning to swim, which helped me with breathing control and upper body strength, and being as active as possible.

I never felt like I was expected to be slower or less robust than the others because of my asthma — I just always did my best to keep up with everyone else. When I was about three, Mum took me to creative dancing classes — that's the first organised class I can remember going to. Me and all the other little kids would flit around pretending to be fairies and have a great time. I absolutely loved it!

Our place was close to the beach so, even if it was raining, Mum would take us down there for a bit of a run around. We all absolutely loved the beach. My two cousins, Kim and Victoria, were a similar age to me so I spent heaps of time hanging out with them when I was a kid.

There was plenty of sibling rivalry between me and Dawson. We used to fight all the time and I absolutely doted on Mitchell. He was my wee baby when I was a kid. I think it was partly because he was quite sick. I used to do whatever I could to protect him from everything.

Getting out and being active was always a part of our family life. Mum was a keen swimmer and skier when she was growing up and Dad was really into his rugby and he was a great player — he made rep teams for both Taranaki and Wanganui. Dad wanted me to be an All Black — it didn't matter that girls didn't play rugby back then. (I think I was born too early!) He always said that to represent your country was the ultimate achievement in sport. He instilled that belief in all of us kids and he pushed us hard to achieve that goal.

Dad played first grade rugby until he was 45 and then he only quit because people kept telling him it was about time — he reckons he was still kicking arse. When he hung up his rugby boots Dad really threw himself into fishing and hunting to fill in his spare time. When we were growing up Dad loved it when the three of us kids all went bush with him. I didn't really enjoy going out hunting. I didn't like killing animals — it's really not in my nature. I would rather cuddle them than kill them. But I would have done anything to make my dad proud. He's just one of those people you really want to make proud. He's got this real mana about him and I hated ever feeling like I'd failed him. So I'd go out and do the very best I could when we were out in the bush together. Secretly, I'd aim over the heads of the animals — not that Dad knew that! It taught me to hang in there when it's cold and I'm tired and scared.

Mum being a teacher meant that we could all read and write a bit before we started school. I was always a really good student and never struggled to keep up in class. I enjoyed primary school and I didn't have to worry about my asthma there as Mum taught at my school. I was a real Mummy's girl and I felt secure knowing that my mum was never more than a call away. In fact, she still is and we are very close.

Once I started school, a whole lot of organised sports were suddenly available to me. At the age of five, I decided that gymnastics was for me. Even after taking me to creative dancing classes, Mum was really relieved that I hadn't picked dancing as she reckoned that it was a bit prissy and wouldn't have suited me. I think she was right. I was definitely a 'rip, shit and bust' kid who couldn't sit still for five minutes.

Even from a young age, I was diligent about going to gym practices and making sure I achieved as much as I could. I was coordinated and quite talented at it but I wasn't exceptional. I remember watching Nadia Comaneci win three gold medals at the 1976 Olympic Games in Montreal. Her perfect 10 on the uneven bars was something else and from that moment on she was my absolute idol. I just wanted to be like her.

Saturday mornings in our household were always really busy with the boys going to rugby and me at gymnastics or netball. Mum and Dad were always very involved in what we were doing and that helped us all to excel. At the same time, they were never pushy.

Dad would follow Dawson's rugby and Mum would be with me at gymnastics. Mitchell was quite sick as a kid as he suffers from coeliac disease so he fitted in around the rest of us a bit.

Between my asthma and Mitchell's coeliac disease, the Tamatis were pretty well known at New Plymouth hospital. Even though Dawson was the healthy one, he was almost fearless and was always doing things like putting his fingers in sockets and jumping off stuff. We must have been a real handful for Mum and Dad!

I was always really determined and even at the age of about ten, there were a few times I'd throw wobblies if things went wrong. I've always pushed myself to be the best and I've always been disappointed when I don't live up to the goals I have set myself.

The fear of dying that came from my asthma meant that at the age of ten, I took myself off to church. I would read the Bible every day and I had lots of rituals that I thought would protect me from dying. I would never step on a crack, I'd have to say prayers if anyone said 'God'. Talcum powder and moisturiser absolutely terrified me — I hated them so much. I reckon that happened because the scent in them could set off an asthma attack. Eventually, that fear of something that could cause an asthma attack became so ingrained that the smell of talc could make me vomit. Looking back, it was really obsessive behaviour for a little kid.

When I was about twelve, I changed from doing sports gymnastics to rhythmic gymnastics and that's when things got tricky for me. Every week we'd get weighed when we went to class and if we put on weight we'd be given a hard time. I started being told that I was too heavy to be a gymnast. I was one of those kids who went through a growth spurt early and I was taller and bigger built than the other girls. It didn't matter that I was a muscular build, all that seemed to matter was being skinny. I was put up with the sixteen year olds at the age of twelve and the expectations that were put on me were huge — I struggled to cope with the pressure that was put on me.

To keep my weight down for gymnastics, I took up running. I'd run a couple of kilometres a day. At the age of twelve, I did a 10-kilometre run on my own.

When I went to high school, I continued to be a diligent student and I played netball and water polo but running wasn't so much a sport for me as a way of keeping fit. I never had a problem being picked for a sports team!

By the age of fourteen I was still one of the top gymnasts in Taranaki and I was competing at national level, but I struggled to break into the elite level of the sport. I knew I didn't have what it took to be in the top five in the country but, even so, I worked really hard to try and do it. I decided to give up gymnastics because the pressure was just too much. As always, Mum was by my side supporting whatever decision I made.

Looking back, those early setbacks have made me even more determined to achieve my goals in later life. Despite the tough times I had before I quit gymnastics, I know that the sport taught me the importance of discipline, training and fitness that has stayed with me for my whole life. I really believe that failing to reach the pinnacle of the gymnastics world taught me a heap of lessons that have enabled me to excel in my chosen sport now. It also helped me realise that even if I didn't have natural ability or talent, I could still achieve anyway.

The boys and I still had our squabbles. I tried to keep the peace between Dawson and Mitchell doing whatever was necessary to stop Dawson from picking on Mitchell. It was a bit of a shock to the system when I became a teenager and decided to take Dawson on in a fight. Suddenly, he was bigger than me and I couldn't beat him up anymore. I was shocked and Mitchell was on his own. Sorry bro!

One year for Christmas, Mum and Dad gave the three of us a surfboard to share. Dad was a bit nervous about the three of us being out on the surfboard. Apart from fishing Dad didn't really like being out in the water but Mum had always been a real water baby so she knew we'd be really into it. We loved it. The three of us got together and hand painted it — it was fantastic! The very first day we went out on it, I jumped on it and it flipped up and hit Mitchell in the head. Once again, the Tamatis were off to hospital — this time so Mitchell could get stitches.

All three of us got really into surfing and the timing couldn't have been better for me. I had plenty of time now I'd given up gymnastics so I threw myself into becoming the best surfer I could. Before long, thankfully, Dawson, Mitchell and I all had our own surfboards. With the beach practically at the bottom of the garden, the three of us were out in the surf every day. For the first two years, we surfed year round without wetsuits. That's how into it we were. I was a bit of a tomboy and I was determined to be as good as Dawson and Mitchell and I knew to do that I had to be tough. I wasn't the most talented surfer but I would go out in the biggest waves, if the boys did. If I got given a wave I'd go over the falls whether I tumbled down the face or I managed to handle it, I'd take it. I put up with the cold and getting hammered by the waves just for the camaraderie and the adventure of it. I loved the adrenaline buzz and I loved jumping in the car with the guys and cruising along the coast looking for waves. Once we were in the water, we'd stay out there until we froze. It's a hard sport. You get beaten around by the waves — in big waves it's like being in a washing machine and often I'd be underwater for what seemed like ages.

Once we were all freezing cold, we'd head home with the music blaring all the way only stopping off to scoff some fish 'n' chips. When you're starving and cold after an afternoon's surfing, they're the best food ever. It sometimes took us a couple of hours to warm up again. I remember for the first couple of years after we got our boards, the three of us used to surf every day, right through winter.

There weren't that many women surfing competitively at that time — I think there were only about four of us in New Plymouth — but I went into all the competitions I could and I thrived on competing against other surfers.

While gymnastics taught me the importance of training and fitness, surfing taught me to never give up and the importance of working through fear for the thrill of a ride. I reckon that's when I first started to harden up a lot.

While surfing took up a lot of my time, I continued to achieve well at school, getting University Entrance and Higher School Certificate as well as being sports captain in my final year. When I finished school, a lot of people thought I'd go to university but I didn't feel ready to leave New Plymouth just yet. I was happy living in Taranaki and I knew that if I went to university I wouldn't be able to spend as much time surfing as I wanted. I got a job at an insurance company alongside my cousin Kim.

I worked there for a year before deciding that being a student might not be such a bad life. I enrolled in some classes in New Plymouth for a year, which meant I could both study and surf. At the end of my first year of study I decided to make the big move up to

Auckland where I enrolled in a business studies course. It was tough being away from home for the first time but I managed to get back home to Taranaki as often as possible.

HITTING THE ROAD

You only do what you think you can do

One day in the middle of December 1994, the rain was absolutely tipping it down in New Plymouth. One of my mates was on his way to my mum's place when he saw this poor tourist on a bike. He did that real Kiwi thing and stopped and offered him a lift and a place to sleep for a night. The tourist was glad of the offer of a dry place to sleep and to be off his bike. They carried on to Mum's place. She was quite taken with this handsome young Austrian tourist called Paul who was spending a few months cycling around New Zealand. He told her that he was going to climb Mount Taranaki the next day and Mum, who has lived in Taranaki her whole life, warned him how dangerous the mountain can be. Paul assured Mum that he was an experienced mountain climber but that didn't convince my mum. Her parting words were, 'Be careful up there, I don't want to hear about you on the radio tomorrow!'

If anyone needs proof that they should listen to their mum (and other people's mums!), that was it. A couple of days later, Mum heard that there was a tourist missing on the mountain. She knew straight away that it was Paul that everyone was up there searching for. He'd gone up the mountain in summer clothes with very little in the way of food and equipment. Even though it was summer, it was cold up the mountain at night and by the next day everyone thought he would be dead. But 36 hours after Paul had gone up the mountain, just before nightfall, the Search and Rescue team found him near the top. He had a badly broken leg with open wounds but apart from that was in good condition. He told his rescuers that he had been hit by a small avalanche, which had pushed him off a bluff.

No one could believe that he was still in such a good condition. Having already wound the rescue team up by going up the mountain completely unprepared, he caused them a bit more grief by trying to take photos of his injuries while the medical team were trying to get him on the helicopter! After being helicoptered off the mountain, Paul was admitted to Taranaki Base Hospital where he began what was to be a lengthy healing and rehabilitation process.

Over the coming months we would learn that this kind of determination and single mindedness was pretty typical of him.

While all this had been going on, I was up in Auckland at university. I got home the day after Paul was admitted to hospital and Mum told me about the young guy she'd met who had had this horrific accident up the mountain. She suggested I go and see him as he had no family or friends around. I was on summer holidays and had nothing better to do so I decided I'd pop in and say hello. I never suspected that my entire life would change as a result of that one visit.

I walked into Paul's hospital room and, even though it sounds a bit cheesy, it was love at first sight. I never actually believed that it could happen but that connection was just there. I thought he was absolutely gorgeous and, at the age of 22 and having lived in New Zealand my whole life, to me he seemed so exotic. I introduced myself and explained that he'd met my mum. He was pretty pleased to have some company so I told him I'd come and see him again the next day.

Paul was in hospital for a few more days and I visited him every day and helped look after him. When it was time for him to be discharged, it was pretty obvious that he wasn't going to be able to look after himself so Mum invited him to come and stay with us. I reckon she had that typical Kiwi thing where she thought that if anything happened to one of her kids overseas, she'd hope that someone would be there to look after them! He was lost, in a foreign country with a broken leg so, of course, she invited him to stay.

Over the next two months, we spent nearly all our time together. Getting to know each other was really intense. He was 21 and had a lot of anger in him. I was a year older than him and our family lives couldn't have been more different. He wasn't close to either of his parents who had divorced when he was quite young. It must have been pretty strange to him when my family scooped him up and decided to look after him. We were, after all, complete strangers and yet he got more unreserved affection and care from us than he had had from his own family.

We used to talk for hours and hours and we played a lot of games like Scrabble. He tried to teach me German. It was a case of doing anything I could to keep his mind occupied. He was such a fit, driven, outdoors person and being unable to get out there just about sent him out of his mind. I was on holiday and had nothing else to do so I looked after him every day. I was completely blown away by all the adventures that he'd had. He was pretty much the same age as me and there he was, biking around the world. He was so exotic and exciting for someone like me who thought the world ended at the beach. Before long we were planning trips that we could do together and we got closer and closer. Soon we were completely in love.

Our relationship started out with me looking after Paul, helping him recover and keeping him occupied. I loved the fact that he needed me so much and he had my complete attention all the time. I spent so much time with him, I hardly had time for surfing or working.

After a couple of months he started to get better but was constantly plagued with ulcers and other side effects. Then I had to make a really tough decision — do I go back to university and carry on my accounting studies in Auckland? Or do I chuck in my studies and stay here with this man from the other side of the world that I've only known for a couple of months?

After a lot of thought, I decided to do the sensible thing and go back to Auckland to finish my degree. That lasted all of two days! By then Paul was getting around on crutches. He came to Auckland to visit me and I realised that our relationship was really important to me. No matter how hard I tried, I couldn't concentrate on my university course, I just wanted to be with Paul and see where the world would take us. I quit my studies and we headed back to Taranaki.

Paul really didn't want to go back to Austria as there was no one there to look after him so he decided to stay in New Plymouth until he had fully recovered. I managed to get a job in an accountant's office where I was in sole charge and we got a flat together and settled into life in New Plymouth.

Our life was pretty normal. I would go to work every day and

Paul focused on his recuperation. It took about a year all up before he was healed enough to go back to doing some of the things he used to do before he was injured. Over that time, we set up house and when I wasn't working we spent all our time together. It was all very exciting. It was the first time either of us had lived with a partner and we had a great time setting up house and planning our future together. Paul spent most of his time working on rehabbing his leg and getting his fitness back.

We spent heaps of time with my family who absolutely loved Paul. They practically adopted him and Mum tried her best to help him heal not only his leg injury but also some of his underlying hurt. Paul and Dad got on really well and he seemed to really want Dad's approval — something we both had in common.

As Paul's leg healed, he started cycling quite a bit. Our first bike trip together was a three-day adventure up to Kawhia, which is about 240 kilometres north of New Plymouth. I had this real old dunger of a bike and I remember thinking it was the hardest thing I'd ever done. I had all my gear in a pack on my back, which was hardly ideal. After about 60 kilometres I felt absolutely wasted but I was determined to prove to Paul that I could keep up with him. I was used to the rough and cold from surfing but this was something else. Even though it was tough going, we had a great time. It felt like such an adventure and I loved sharing it with Paul.

After about eight months, Paul had to go back to Austria to renew his visa and to see his mother. Before he left we got engaged. It wasn't one of those traditional, down on one knee engagements. He was leaving the country and I planned to follow him. We were both frightened of being apart so we decided that we'd get married. He bought me a ring and we spent our last night together at Dawson

Falls, a romantic alpine retreat complete with tin bath and four poster bed, on Mt Taranaki.

Paul left for Austria and was away for a couple of months. I carried on working and tried to go on with my life as normal but I missed him terribly. Even though we'd talked about me following Paul to Austria he decided he wanted to come back to New Zealand.

By the time Paul got back, his leg had healed enough for him to continue his travels around New Zealand. While he was away, I'd tried to save as much money as I could so that we could take off together and see a bit more of the country. Paul planned a trip around the South Island for us so we could explore a bit and then make some money picking fruit. I was looking forward to the pair of us working together as we hated being separated for more than two minutes. He had so much experience in the outdoors and travelling that I had absolutely no problem in letting him do all the planning. I couldn't wait to get back out on the road with Paul.

While it all seemed like a great idea, the reality for me was pretty tough. I still had my old dunger of a bike and my gear was shocking. There was none of the flash lightweight wet-weather gear — I had a bright yellow heavy PVC parka and pants! Compared to Paul, I was in over my head. Biking all day on a crappy bike, trying to keep up with Paul meant that I was exhausted a lot of the time.

Paul expected a lot and I found it hard going. I was surf fit, gym fit but not bike fit. We'd have some major arguments but we were still in that in-love phase and would always make up.

Despite the hardships we had, we did have a lot of fun. We scored a job at an apple orchard near Motueka. We had a caravan on the orchard to live in but it was a few weeks before the apples were ready to pick. We left our gear in the caravan and decided we'd explore the top half of the South Island. We biked all around Marlborough and Canterbury but it wasn't easy going.

While we were on the road, Paul and I would never pay for accommodation. Some nights I found it quite scary to be sleeping out in the open, especially when we were just sleeping on the side of the road. Paul was used to it and he didn't really get why I was being a wimp. On one of the first nights — we weren't that far from Motueka — Paul decided we were going to sleep in a barn. Being a bit of a goody two shoes, I was really worried that the farmer would find us and get shitty. Of course, the next morning, the farmer did turn up. I was really embarrassed but Paul wasn't ready to get up so stayed in his sleeping bag. Luckily, the farmer just laughed. He just said 'gidday' and carried on with whatever it was he was doing.

Paul's main aim was to see as much of the world as possible and he really wanted to show me the world the way he saw it. But, this was my first big bike trip and I found it exhausting. It took ages for my body to get used to being on the bike for long periods of time. My knees were playing up heaps, my back was sore, my Achilles tendons ached and my bum was killing me from being on the bike seat. I'd be head down, bum up concentrating on cycling and Paul would be taking in all the scenery and loving it. He could see I wasn't finding it easy and I think he found that really frustrating.

One of the toughest days of the trip was the 124 kilometres through the mountains to get to Hanmer Springs. When we finally arrived at Hanmer Springs I was knackered — my Achilles tendons were screaming. Sinking into the hot pools at Hanmer was absolute luxury. Moments like that made the whole trip worthwhile.

Near Hanmer Springs, we went to an adventure playground and decided to play on all the flying foxes, rope walks and stuff. We were having a great time skylarking around when I decided to get onto a flying fox. It was a pretty big one but it wasn't until I was flying along on it that I realised that it was a kids' one and I was probably a bit too heavy for it. I was going way too fast. When I got to the other end, I hit the tyre that was supposed to stop me and it threw me two metres up in the air upside–down and slammed me against a tree. The tree stopped the flying fox, but didn't stop me; I kept going and fell head first to the ground. I really hurt my back.

Throughout the trip, Paul had constantly instilled in me the need to toughen up and just carry on. I didn't want to disappoint him and I didn't want him to think that I was weak so I got up about five minutes later and biked off despite being in a lot of pain. I could still walk but I was in agony. Later, my back turned black and blue. Paul had absolutely no patience so I felt that I had no choice but to get up and get on with it.

I had really severe bruising and my back hurt like hell but I didn't think to see a doctor about it — I just took Paul's advice and tried to work through it. Eventually Paul said, 'You're bloody hopeless at biking so maybe you might be a bit less crap at tramping.' So, we headed back to Motueka to drop off our bikes. As soon as we'd dumped our bikes and reorganised our packs we hitched down to Invercargill and then on to Bluff to catch the ferry to Stewart Island to do some tramping. But this wasn't going to be your average Sunday stroll. Paul had decided that we'd walk the tracks that circumnavigate Stewart Island.

We got the ferry from Bluff and pitched up at Halfmoon Bay ready to do the northwest and southern circuit tracks on the island. Combined, the nearly 200 kilometres of track take about 12 days to complete. The terrain varies from steep, slippery tracks to exposed coastal trails where you're belted by spray from the ocean. These two tracks, but especially the northwest circuit, are some of the most difficult in the country and are recommended only for fit, well-equipped, experienced trampers. I was none of these things.

We loaded up on supplies and, as we both ate like horses, the backpacks weighed around 25 kilograms each. My badly injured back didn't really need to be lugging that around for days on end.

The weather was absolutely treacherous and the beauty of being out in the untouched wilderness was somewhat tempered by the abundance of mud. Some days we'd be dragging our way through mud almost up to our waists.

Once we were about halfway around the island, we found out that the second half of the track was under even more water than the first and at some points it was almost impassable. This, combined with the fact that I was in excruciating pain because of my back, meant that we decided to turn around and head back the way we came. We'd failed to complete a planned trip again and it was all my fault.

Paul planned everything to such detail that he hated giving up. Even though he'd spent so much time planning and trying to achieve goals, Paul always really enjoyed everything on his trips. He managed to take in every detail of what we were seeing and doing. He loved seeing new birds and trees — he was just such a nature boy. In the great outdoors, Paul was in his element. Even though I'd grown up out in the bush with my dad, Paul's vast knowledge of the natural world sometimes made me feel like a total townie.

When we had run out of time on Stewart Island we caught the ferry back to Bluff then spent three days hitching lifts back to Motueka. The caravan we had to live in on the orchard was really dirty and crappy and Paul and I weren't exactly ideal employees. He had a completely stuffed leg and found it tough to stand on ladders and pick apples all day and my back was still agonising. To top that off, I'm not the most co-ordinated of people and I kept falling off the ladder while I was stretching to get to fruit on high branches!

At the start of the season you had to pick just the ripe fruit so that took quite a bit of practice. Later in the season, when you had to strip the trees completely, we made a bit more money. We had hoped to save a lot so we could pay for Paul to go to Australia to get a special type of reconstructive therapy for his leg, which hadn't healed properly. But, our combined injuries meant that we were only earning about two dollars an hour because we were being paid by the kilo of apples picked. It took us about thirteen hours a day picking apples to make enough money just to live on so we didn't get to save much. It was pretty hopeless and it wasn't long before we realised we weren't going to make our fortune in the apple orchard!

After the second time I fell off the ladder, I felt a bit weird but got up and carried on. The next morning, I went to put a piece of toast in the toaster and everything went black. When I came to, Paul told me that I'd had a major seizure. I'd never had anything like that before and there's no history of epilepsy in my family so I was pretty freaked out.

Paul took me to see a doctor and I told him what had happened. He told me that I'd probably strained my back apple-picking and didn't send me for X-rays. I figured he was probably right because I certainly wasn't used to having 20 kilograms of apples hanging off me for most of the day! The doctor prescribed ten days bed rest for me and sent me back to the caravan.

I spent two weeks lying in that filthy, damp caravan while Paul would go out and try to pick enough apples to support both of us. I couldn't move for the first few days. Every little movement was agonising. It would take me about three hours to get up, get out of the caravan and over to the shower block to go to the toilet or have a shower.

After a couple of weeks, I managed to walk again and went back to picking apples. I was still in a lot of pain but I figured the doctor had been right and it was just a bad strain. Paul and I carried on picking until the end of the season and, even though we had managed to save quite a bit of money, we hadn't completed any of the expeditions that Paul had set out to achieve. The trip had been a failure so we hitched back to New Plymouth.

When I got back, I decided I'd better go to the doctor again. It had been about two and a half months since I'd had the accident at Hanmer Springs and my back was still giving me a lot of grief. Once I explained everything to my doctor, he told me to get straight to the hospital and get my back X-rayed. The results of the test were an absolute shock. My L2 and L3 vertebrae were both fractured — my back was broken!

Thankfully my spinal cord was OK, but two vertebrae had been fractured and two discs were compressed. It was pretty frightening to find out that I was mere millimetres away from being in a wheelchair for the rest of my life — and I'd spent all that time working in the orchard, carrying massive amounts of fruit and falling off ladders.

Now that I'd been diagnosed I was faced with a really tough decision. I could either get the vertebrae fused in order to relieve some of the pressure on my back or I could just put up with the pain and slowly try to strengthen up the muscles around it while the bones healed. I was pretty matter of fact about it and decided to get on with rehabbing my back. I never really dwelled on the injury too much. I chose, instead, to focus on the fact that I was bloody lucky to still be able to walk.

By the time I found out what had happened the bones had already started to set and after a lot of soul searching I decided to let nature take its course. I was only 22 and I couldn't really face the idea of having a fused back at such a young age. Although one of the things the doctor did say to me while I was making my decision was that I shouldn't run at all, that I should keep the jarring on my spine to an absolute minimum and that I should never lift anything heavy. At that stage I was more into biking than running anyway so it didn't really worry me.

The pain from that injury is still with me as I have the compressed discs and quite bad arthritis in my back but it's one of those things you get used to. Ironically, it doesn't bother me nearly as much when I'm running as when I'm biking yet it was because I spend so much time on my bike that I decided not to get the operation done. But then, I reckon everyone's got something that holds them back. I figure this is mine and I just have to get over it. At least I've still got my legs — I had the choice of giving up and becoming a couch potato but that wasn't me. It would have been so easy for me to sit down and go, 'Nah, I can't do it anymore', but I was always on a mission and couldn't sit still for five minutes. I worked around the pain as best I could.

Despite the seriousness of my injuries, Paul didn't give me much sympathy. He still reckoned I should just suck it up and carry on as if nothing had happened. It was pretty hurtful because Paul was still suffering from the side effects of his time on Mt Taranaki. His foot still hadn't healed properly and it was giving him a lot of grief.

But I was very much in love and I would have done anything to make him happy. He was the kind of person who didn't like to be restricted in any way. The injury made him really grumpy — he was 21 and reckoned his life was over. I now believe he also suffered from depression as a result. We'd heard about this reconstructive therapy that a doctor in Sydney was doing so we used all our savings to send him across the Tasman to try and get his foot fixed with this so-called revolutionary new treatment.

Unfortunately, for both of us, the treatment didn't help. He was meant to be as fit as he could be to undertake the treatment and when the medical team did preliminary tests, they found that Paul was suffering from hepatitis, which he must have contracted at the orchard. Paul was devastated.

By the time he got back from Sydney, things between us were pretty shaky. We'd spent all our savings on therapy that didn't work and Paul was getting more bitter and more angry about the lot that he'd been dealt in life. Despite his behaviour getting more extreme and his desire to control me becoming more obvious, I still believed that our relationship could improve and that he loved me. I couldn't see that things were progressively getting worse.

Paul hated the materialism that he'd been brought up with and was determined to live a very different life to that of his childhood. I think that was why he loved the outdoors so much. All he cared about was animals and nature. I really looked up to his moral stances — he was anti-cars and anti-industry. Paul was an extreme environmentalist, the first I'd met, and I really admired him for that. I admired the fact that he'd travelled the world and I loved that he cared so much about animals and nature. It didn't take long before I was hooked on the idea of having a life like that. Paul offered me that life and a whole lot of excitement and exotic experiences to boot. For the adventures that he promised I was willing to overlook some of the less palatable things about our relationship. My confidence and self-esteem took a constant battering.

Even after I did all the things he wanted so that I was as green and as environmentally conscious as him, it still wasn't enough. He believed I was only doing things to please him and he'd tell me I didn't care enough about the planet. I wasn't ever quite good enough.

Getting started

When you start running, you can't go at it like a bull at a gate. Your cardiovascular system will adapt more quickly than your ligaments and tendons and bones, so even though you might be fit you can't force your body to cope. When you first start out you're likely to get inflammation in your knees and your ankles — don't give up too early. You need to give your body time to adjust to the new exercise regime. Ease into it. Three or four times a week for 30 to 40 minutes is a reasonable start. The key is regularity not level of difficulty. Getting a good base of fitness is the first goal.

CORSICA? COURSE I CAN

----

*To try something is to risk failure but not to try
is to guarantee it*

After we'd both spent just over a year trying to recuperate, Paul
decided it was time for him to go back to Austria. And, of course,
he wanted me to go with him. I was excited about seeing the world
with Paul. My parents both loved Paul, too, and really supported my
decision to go off travelling with him. They never saw his controlling
behaviour and didn't suspect how unbalanced our relationship was.
Paul went back first and I followed him a couple of months later.

Looking back, I was pretty green. It was my first time on an
aeroplane, let alone my first time out of the country. I was absolutely
terrified but Paul had no understanding of my concerns — he'd
travelled so much that my fear of being in a place where I didn't
speak the language, so far away from my family and where I didn't
know anyone was completely bizarre to him. Where most people

in that situation would get support and understanding from their partners, Paul couldn't understand that because I hadn't been out of New Zealand before I found the idea of moving to Vienna was pretty overwhelming. It didn't matter to me though because I was determined to make our relationship work.

Paul met me at the airport in Vienna and we went back to his tiny 30-square-metre flat — our new home. It was scarcely big enough for one person so we lived right on top of each other. We had no time apart at all and things sometimes got a bit heated. The apartment building we lived in, which was owned by Paul's mother, was in a quite slummy district and we shared the building with a lot of recent immigrants and refugees.

It was a total shock to the system for me having come from living in a big house by the sea in New Plymouth to having a flat the size of our old kitchen, with a toilet that was outside in a shared hallway. Despite its tiny size the flat felt like home for me. Once I got behind those doors I felt safe and happy — I was living with the man I loved and I was going to make it work!

All the things that had come so easily to me in New Zealand were just that little bit harder for me in Austria. Going to the supermarket and not recognising anything was exciting and challenging at the same time. Our life together completely revolved around planning for our next trip. He never lived in the present, everything was all about the next cycle tour, the next country, the next mission. At the flat, space was taken up with maps on the floor as we planned the best routes, worked out where he hadn't been before and how to get from one place to the next as cheaply as possible.

I'd only been in Vienna a couple of weeks before we were out on the road again. Our first trip in Europe together was to be two months cycling around western Europe, starting in Corsica in April. We had drawn a line on our map showing the route, starting with a trip around the island of Corsica and then on to northern Italy, the Swiss and Austrian Alps and home to Vienna. Paul, the experienced bike tourist, had assured me it would be a piece of cake. The fact that the route included twelve passes above 2000 metres and countless smaller ones, at a time of year when it wasn't exactly warm was, according to Paul, no reason for concern. April is a little early for a cycling tour of Corsica, but we never let a little thing like bad weather stop us. Not Paul and me, well, I just went along for the ride.

We caught an overnight train from Vienna through Italy to Nice. Everything we did was on a really tight budget so we didn't pay for a sleeper and our second class seats were right next to a couple of Italian gentlemen who had no trouble sleeping. Their snoring kept us both awake so we arrived in the French port of Nice sleep deprived and eager to get on with the trip.

To get to Corsica we loaded ourselves and our bikes onto a ship for a midnight sailing out of Nice. When it came to buying tickets there was no way we were going to splash out on a cabin. Paul reckoned we'd be OK sleeping on the deck for the overnight sailing. I was fresh off the plane and had no idea so I just went along with what he said, just as I had ever since we first met.

It was calm and warm when we left Nice at midnight. But by 4.30 in the morning, the wind had started to get up and was increasing in strength with each passing minute. I poked my nose out of my sleeping bag — was it raining? No, but water was pouring over the deck and it was sea water, even though we were four storeys up. Paul woke up and tried frantically to keep a hold of everything. He pulled himself up on a rail, swung his backpack on his back and his sleeping bag under his arm and disappeared into the dark.

I crawled out of my sleeping bag and quickly tried to jam everything into my pack. The ship lurched and my shoe skidded across the deck stopping under a rail and my sleeping bag cover was picked up and blown away by the wind. I stood up, slipped and fell. The strength of the wind was overwhelming. Turning my back against it, I fumbled my way down some stairs and along a rail. In the next second Paul was beside me and helped me through a door. I dropped everything on the floor and sat down feeling dazed, cold, wet and windblown. After a few moments I realised we were not alone — we had entered the crew's quarters and some amused sailors asked us if everything was all right. 'Yeah, yeah', we said. 'No problem.'

No problem except I only had one shoe and it was one half of the only pair I'd brought with me. Paul tried without success to recover the other one. By 6 am the ship was coming into the port of Bastia and the wind was no longer so violent. It took a couple more attempts and, eventually, I was reunited with my shoe.

When we finally docked at Bastia, Paul and I jockeyed with cars and trucks to get off the ship first. There was no way we wanted to be stuck in the belly of the ship behind four hundred or so cars with their motors running. We managed to get away pretty quickly but I wasn't too interested in the sights and sounds of Bastia. All that interested me right now was a bed or, at least, a piece of flat ground to lie down on. It took 20 kilometres of biking, a visit to a supermarket and two photography stops before we found a place to camp. For the rest of the day we lay unconscious in our tent, glad to be protected from the wind storm that was continuing outside. This was one of the rare times that Paul would break from his daily goal of cycling 100 kilometres a day. When he set himself a goal like that he hated missing it so he must have been as knackered as I was just that once.

Next morning the clouds were threatening and the wind was still strong. One day later than planned, our tour began. The riding was cold but refreshing so I soon recovered from our sleepless nights. The road wound its way through coastal villages staying close by the sea before we rounded the top of Cap Corse and came down onto the west side of the spit, where a steeper and more rugged coastline awaited us.

We passed through a number of villages set high up on the mountainside that looked like ghost towns, with empty houses with boarded up doors, and old people wandering along the narrow streets or sitting at tables outside their houses chatting. Centuries-old villages were dying out — no work, no money — and youth were moving to the cities. We saw this trend all over the island. Everything and everyone looked a bit tired.

The road was hilly, very narrow and set hair-raisingly high on the cliff. Luckily there wasn't much traffic but when something came it was often a truck or a bus that left just enough room for us to squeeze by. Unhappily, we were on the right-hand side, with a vertical drop down to the deep blue sea a couple of hundred feet below. Dotted along the roadside we saw many car wrecks on the cliffs, again something we saw all over Corsica. The roads were dangerous and had obviously claimed many a life. We counted fifteen wrecks in one valley — a warning to take it easy.

After a few hours on the road, we'd always be pretty hungry. Food was fuel and we were on a tight budget so we used to cook our own meals on the side of the road. A regular favourite on the menu was my speciality, Salmon Lisi — tomato sauce, spaghetti and a can of tuna (salmon was too expensive for our budget) prepared on our trusty little gas cooker. It amazes me how something so simple can taste so good when you've been biking out in the cold all day. There was only one problem — I could have devoured the whole pot myself. There was never enough. Food was just another thing I let Paul control.

With a half full tummy we climbed up the next steep pass, puffing hard. Until my body had regained its rhythm and warmed up and as I struggled up a particularly nasty little stretch, I wondered if I was serious about completing the planned two month tour. Had I overestimated myself? We'd been looking forward to this tour for months, my first big trip, and on paper it had looked good. Only a couple of days in and already I wasn't quite so sure.

The night was approaching as we neared the end of Cap Corse. It was our policy to travel as far as possible for as little as possible and to rarely pay for accommodation so we found a sheltered spot on the beach to set up camp for the night. When we were camping we never had a fire and always left things as we found them. We disturbed no one and we saved ourselves a lot of money.

Next morning the mountains behind us were sprinkled with snow, the air was moist and chilly and our rollercoaster ride along the coast continued until we reached the pretty town of St Florent, a touristy harbour village with more hotels than houses and a shop with the freshest French bread in the world. After an hour sitting in the sun we turned inland, toward the mountains. The first highlight of the tour wasn't far away — the 35-kilometre long Asco valley is a one-way road that ends at the ski resort of Mt Cinto 1400 metres above sea level.

The way up was long and winding, after 20 kilometres the

proper road ended and we found ourselves on a pot-holed, half-sealed–half-metalled road. It was beautiful and peaceful up there in the mountains. Not a soul around and only the sound of my rhythmical breathing to keep me company. Before long I saw the ski field at the top of the road. Everything was closed for the season so we were alone. We were surrounded by majestic snow-capped mountains, the highest being Mt Cinto at 2707 metres. After a short break we went for a walk before heading back down to the valley below. Wrapped up in four layers of clothing, including my favourite yellow PVC to keep the chill and the wind out, I enjoyed the speed of the ride down. Tired and happy we made it just before dark.

Next day we arrived in the town of Corte. It's a pretty town and because it was raining we decided to book into a very strange but cheap camping ground where there were no showers and the toilets were locked. In the early morning, Paul stuck the thermometer outside the tent — it was zero degrees. Despite my winter sleeping attire of two pairs of socks, two pairs of thermal underwear, tracksuit pants, two T-shirts, a sweatshirt, jacket, hat, ski gloves and my sleeping bag, I was freezing.

Eventually I convinced my cold body to get moving. The day's ride was not an easy one, pass after pass came at us, and I started to feel a little seasick on the up-and-down rollercoaster. By the time we reached the top of our last pass for the day it had started to snow so we took the next road down towards the coast, where it was much warmer.

Our next goal on the map was Bonifacio. We strolled through the old city with its narrow cobblestone alleys that run between the high castle-like apartments, quaint boutiques and romantic cafes and restaurants. Nothing so extravagant for us! That night we slept in a small concrete shelter, escaping the storm that raged all night and through the next morning. We waited until 10.30 am for a break in the weather before breaking camp to get back on the road. Too soon the rain was back, so we hurriedly packed up and biked through the old part of the town and got stuck behind a funeral procession. It must have made quite a sight — 150 or so people dressed in black, all very mournful and sad, followed closely by two yellow-PVC clad bike tourists impatiently but respectfully bringing up the rear. After 20 minutes following the procession we realised we had gone round in a circle.

By 6.30 that night we had to start looking for a place to sleep. After going through a few possibilities Paul reckoned he'd found the perfect place. 'Up there behind that little church, we will be hidden from the road.' Well, he said church — I say cemetery. There was no way in hell I was sleeping in a cemetery, especially having spent a chunk of my day following a funeral procession. No matter that it was sheltered from the road, it was not going to happen and I told Paul so. Uncharacteristically, Paul gave in and we ended up sleeping in the field next door. There was only a fence separating us from the graveyard but at least we were not in there! I'm not superstitious but I don't believe in pushing your luck.

Before we knew it our last night in Corsica had arrived. In the 17 days we spent in Corsica we climbed over 9000 metres in height — that's more than the equivalent of going from sea level to the top of Mt Everest. On that last night, as we were on our way back into Bastia and it was getting dark, I was worried that we wouldn't have anywhere to sleep for the night. As the outer suburbs rolled past, Paul spotted a half-built house — at least it offered us half a roof over our heads and, perhaps, a chance to dry out. I would have given anything to have been dry and warm.

The bare concrete floor didn't look very inviting so Paul and I put the tent up. Inside the tent it was always a little warmer and it felt like home to me, my bedroom if you like. No matter how horrible things were outside, in my tent I felt at home and comfortable. It's amazing how little comforts and a routine can help you feel at home. So, the tent became my little house that night. But it was to be anything but comfortable.

At 9 pm the owner of the half-built house paid us a surprise visit. We were embarrassed to be caught on his land without permission and thought he'd kick us off. Thankfully, he took pity on us and let us stay. I was so relieved that I think he got a bit sick of hearing me say 'Merci, merci, merci' about a hundred times, but our troubles weren't over. We retired to our beds early and fell quickly asleep as the rain that had taunted us throughout Corsica returned with a vengeance. Eventually water started to pour down from a hole in the roof and, after half an hour, we were wet through from the rain and frozen cold. I looked outside the tent and saw we were lying in a pool of water — there was going to be no respite from the wet.

After a shocking night's sleep and waking up in a lake of water, we arrived in the city and found a warm, sunny spot in the middle of a square where a market was being set up. We proceeded to empty out our bags and spread all our gear out to dry — sleeping bags, tents, clothing, the lot. I think some people thought we were opening up a stall. I was pretty relieved to be able to pack up sun-dried gear and get on the ferry to Italy. Thankfully, the return trip was somewhat calmer than our first ferry ride.

We arrived in Genoa late that afternoon. I'd have given anything for a soft mattress and a roof over my head, but it was not to be. Our first night in Italy was spent in an abandoned factory in the middle of the city. It was pretty creepy so we slept with our bikes chained to our hands, just in case. The southern part of Italy is so densely populated that we decided to take a train north to get to some less-populated Italian roads. It turned out to be a good choice as Italy had suffered from terrible flooding over the previous week and huge swathes of land were underwater.

Near the border with Switzerland the pass we wanted to travel over was closed due to snow. Paul was having none of it. He said, 'That's fine, we'll just climb over the fence and we'll carry the bikes up'. As usual Miss Party Pooper was feeling panicky and scared and made sure Paul knew it. He had no fear of anything and he hated that I wouldn't just do what he said — he had no mercy when it came to my fear. Surrounded by snow, we had a huge fight but I put my foot down. There was no way I was going up a closed pass when no one knew where we were. I got my way.

In the end, we took another train to a town called Chur in Switzerland. Paul was furious but I took it because I was happy not to be lost in the mountains and we spent the night on what would have been a romantic spot on the Rhine River but for the fact that Paul was barely speaking to me.

The following morning, we were back on our bikes and heading for Lake Constance, a beautiful lake that lies on the border between Germany, Switzerland and Austria. We'd only been on the road for 20 minutes before . . . CRASH! A stick had got jammed through the forks of my front wheel and had ripped all the spokes out and bent the frame. The impact had sent me flying over the handlebars and I was lying flat on my back in the dirt with a terrible pain in my left arm and a badly mangled bike.

Paul slammed on his brakes in order to avoid a collision, dropped his bike and ran over to me. I was lying on the ground groaning in pain. 'It's my arm', I managed to say. Paul, for once, looked panicked, 'It looks bad — it's sticking out funny'. Comforting words, indeed!

I told Paul to go and find a doctor. First he took a couple of photos of me lying there in agony — taking photos was his major preoccupation on all trips. Him and his bloody camera! I just lay there feeling shocked and at the same time worrying that I'd ruined the rest of the trip.

After what seemed like ages, Paul came back with a doctor who took me to his clinic in a local village. He examined my arm, took X-rays and delivered the unsurprising verdict– my arm was broken. The doctor couldn't put a plaster on it and gave us instructions on how to get to the nearest hospital. He added for good measure, 'Don't move your arm. A small piece of bone is only just hanging on and if it breaks you could have a permanently stiff arm.'

The hospital was 15 kilometres away. Each step I took shook my arm a little and I was not happy about risking a permanently stiff arm. Having just arrived from Italy, we had no Swiss money so, instead of taking the bus, Paul went into a church and asked if someone could help us. A kindly gentleman offered to take us to the hospital and an hour later the plaster was on and an operation was deemed unnecessary. Feeling a little depressed we boarded the train home to Vienna. Paul was really disappointed about the trip ending prematurely because he'd really wanted to show me more of Europe.

Back home in Vienna, it wasn't long before Paul was making travel plans for us again. It didn't matter to him that my arm was broken. He reckoned I could still walk with my arm in plaster so after just two days back at the flat, we set off to the Schneealpe, a

1900-metre high mountain with multiple peaks, at the end of the limestone alps range not far from Vienna. Typically, Paul decided that the most straightforward way up the mountain was not the best way. I found myself clambering over bushes and running up scoria slopes single-handedly.

I so wanted Paul to be happy with me that I risked further and more-permanent damage to my arm. All I wanted was for him to think I was good enough and to be able to see the world the way he wanted me to see it. Even though I managed to climb the mountain and get back down safely, it wasn't enough. I still felt useless. I wasn't fast enough. I wasn't tough enough.

I felt like I would never measure up. Paul could handle so much pain and cold. I couldn't and yet I'd over-train and struggle quietly to cope. I'd get depressed and Paul would just get more and more pissed off with me. He couldn't understand why I couldn't just be happy, despite his criticism of me. He'd get pissed off with me for not looking around and enjoying the view when we were biking. As if I could enjoy the view when I was head down over my pedals puffing my lungs out climbing another mountain pass. Things should have got easier as I got fitter but it never really happened.

Paul eventually admitted that I wasn't a bad cyclist. I was stoked. But then he followed up by telling me that I was an absolutely useless runner and would never be any good. He said I shouldn't even try to run — famous last words. That's still his opinion today, despite everything that I've done! I guess that just proves that nothing I could have done would have impressed him. He was as hard on me as he was on himself. His favourite saying was 'It's just the truth — not a relative opinion.'

When we were back in Vienna, I decided to step up my training so I could keep up with him. I'd run most days and Paul took every opportunity to tell me how useless I was. He reckoned I wasn't built for running and that I should just give up. He sure knew exactly how to push my buttons — all the insecurities I'd developed would come straight to the surface. Still, if there's one thing I'll never do, it's give up. No matter what Paul said to me, I was determined to improve and prove it to him that I wasn't hopeless.

Our outing to the Schneealpe didn't sate Paul's wanderlust. As soon as my arm was out of plaster, he decided it was time for our next bike trip. Too bad that I wasn't supposed to put any weight on my arm and that I was supposed to take it easy for a while.

Paul spent hours planning our trips. The floor of our tiny apartment was, as usual, covered in maps and he planned everything to the tiniest detail. I was so impressed that he knew so much about so many places and I had hardly seen anything. Whenever Paul was planning a trip, he'd encourage me to come up with my own ideas for a trip that we could do. I thought about it but I soon realised that whatever I suggested, he had a hundred trips of his own waiting to be planned. In the end, I realised that there was no point in reinventing the wheel and let him get on with it.

4

SCANDINAVIA BY BIKE
----

*Develop a curiosity about all that is new and exciting
in the world*

The next trip Paul planned was through Scandinavia on our bikes. We
were going to be on the road for two months and would cover 3500
kilometres. Thankfully, it was going to be in the summer so we left
Vienna in June.

When we got to Stockholm to start the trip, I was scared. I didn't
know how my arm would hold up and this was going to be the first
really long-distance trip for me. To add to that we didn't have good
bikes and our gear was pretty archaic because we did everything on
the cheap.

My hopes for warm summer days cruising through meadows
of flowers with not a care in the world evaporated pretty much as
soon as we left Stockholm. Even though it was mid-summer, I hadn't
really factored that Sweden is a country that spends much of its time

under snow with temperatures in winter averaging between –13° to –18° Celsius. For the first week of the trip, it rained intermittently. Then for the next three weeks it rained solidly day and night. The land was green and lush and the temperature was above freezing so this qualified as summer in Sweden.

Despite the inclement weather, Paul remained determined to cover the requisite 100 kilometres a day. By night ten of the trip, we'd covered 1028 kilometres. We'd been through scenery that consisted of little more than miles and miles of pine tree plantations. Something that's pretty familiar to people from the central North Island, it just didn't seem that different or exciting.

Our sleeping places were usually somewhere on the side of the road in the middle of nowhere, surrounded by trees. Everything we had with us was wet, dirty and starting to go mouldy. The thought of another six weeks of this was too much. All I wanted was a hot shower and clean clothes — my ambitions had been downgraded somewhat since I'd wished for a warm bed in Corsica.

I remember one night that was so wet that Paul couldn't get the camp stove going. He tried for ages to cook our last can of beans and in the end, he gave up. He crawled in beside me bearing soggy, lukewarm baked beans and we ate in silence. What on earth were we doing there? Sure we had no work, no responsibilities, no timetables and were in a beautiful country, but there had to be more to life than mouldy polypropylenes and a stinky PVC raincoat and freezing our arses off.

Thankfully before long the landscape began to change. The trees thinned and gave way to hardy alpine plants and grasses in a rocky landscape. One of the highlights for me was when we passed into the Arctic Circle. For a kid from Taranaki, that was pretty exciting. The Arctic Circle is in Lapland, which is an ancient region that takes in the north of Norway, Sweden and Finland. It is the home of the Sami people, a reindeer-herding, nomadic people who have inhabited this area for thousands of years. The climate is particularly harsh in winter when it's dark for two whole months and in summer the sun never sets. We were in the land of the midnight sun!

It was a really strange experience to wake at three in the morning and find it as bright as day. On the downside, it meant we could ride our bikes all night and, of course, Paul was keen that we do just that. It was an amazing experience riding along a deserted road watching the midnight sun, the changing shades of pinks and reds, the mist moving like a ghost over the lakes and rivers, and once in a while the fleeting glimpse of a polar fox or moose, always with the hope of seeing one of the elusive brown bears who love to roam there at night. We only ever caught a fleeting glimpse of a bear but they were nevertheless a cause for concern because every night we had to sleep in their territory.

Not long after we passed the circle marker we made it to the town of Jokkmokk. There we swapped our bikes for backpacks and spent two weeks hiking. Our first hike was in Padjelanta National Park. We'd been invited to visit a summer reindeer camp by a Sami woman we met along the way and we were looking forward to experiencing something of the Sami way of life. All up the trek was supposed to take us 10 days. But before we'd even made it to the first camp, we ran into trouble.

It was only our second day in the park and we were on our way up to the highest point. Ahead of us lay melting snow and because of all the recent rain, a couple of the rivers ahead of us were in flood meaning difficult river crossings were on the cards. We were not particularly well equipped.

At about 6 pm a rare patch of fine weather broke and it started to pour with rain again. We erected the tent on a swampy plateau and climbed on in. We ended up staying in there for nearly three days! The storm lashed and whipped its way around us, but our wee tent stood steadfast throughout. It was leaking, propped up and stuck down with extra sticks and bags. But nonetheless it remained standing and probably saved our lives. Even though it was scary, that enforced time in the tent was the best rest I'd had in ages so I decided to make the most of it.

After two nights the storm eased and we finally got out of the tent. Surprisingly, during the enforced time in the tent, Paul and I got on better than we had for a while. It was probably because we didn't have to do anything. I wasn't trying to keep up with him and he had no choice but to stay there.

Once the storm eased we had to walk back the way we had come because we didn't have the provisions to make it to the other end of the trail. On top of that there was the prospect of icy river crossings, so we trudged the 55 kilometres back to the road. We never made it to the summer reindeer camp. Paul was really disappointed.

About halfway back to the road, we came across a school group being taken up the pass by a teacher. Paul went and told him not to take the kids across the pass as it was dangerous. The school teacher wasn't having a bar of it. The whole group was ill-equipped and inexperienced. I still can't believe that teacher's attitude to the outdoors and I wouldn't have been surprised to hear that some of those kids got into real trouble. I just don't get that people don't listen when they're warned about bad conditions in the outdoors.

After we got back to the road, it only took us a few hours to restock our supplies and bike to Muddus National Park just up the road. Here we'd planned a 60-kilometre tramp through the bush over the next few days. That leisurely plan soon got scuppered. As soon as we got off our bikes, we were absolutely swarmed by thousands of bloodthirsty mosquitoes. I've never seen anything like it. I reckon they could have drained both of us in minutes if we'd stood still. As it is half swamp and half forest, Muddus was a veritable breeding ground for the little blighters. There was stagnant water everywhere and the mozzies loved it. We decided that the only thing for it was to go as fast as we could — if you stopped you were dinner. Going to the toilet was the absolute worst. As soon as you dropped your pants, your bottom would be covered in mozzie bites within seconds.

There was only one hut on the track at about the 25-kilometre mark and we literally ran to get there. As soon as we got there we slammed the door and hoped like hell we hadn't let too many in. We killed all the mozzies we could find and cowered indoors for a few hours. It suddenly made sense why some of the animals we had seen had been sitting in the last little patches of snow in the forest — they were trying to keep away from the mozzies!

We ending up running the whole track and we completed the 60 kilometres in just under one and a half days. We'd been so focused on avoiding getting bitten that we hardly saw a thing except the ground passing under our feet and the mosquitoes.

About two thirds of the way along the track there was a viewing platform where you could stand and watch the midnight sun. Above the tree line and the mosquitoes, Paul set up his camera and took a series of photos of the sun moving across the sky. It was magic — a night I'll never forget.

Our next walk took us to the top of the highest mountain in Sweden, Kebnekaise. It was a beautiful day as we headed off on the final climb to the top. As we were climbing a steep snowfield I heard a loud rumbling over to my right — avalanche! Just 100 metres away from us a cloud of snow was rushing down the field. I froze in fear and hoped that by walking up the snowfield we wouldn't start another avalanche above us. To my eternal relief the snow stayed solid and we reached the summit safely. The views from the top were magnificent and we sat for an hour on the summit enjoying the peace and the beautiful panorama below.

In the evening we returned to our tent after a good day to find a fox had paid a visit. It had ripped the side of the tent open in an effort to get our food. We were not at all amused but thankfully he was gone by the time we got back and at least he wasn't a bear! We managed to get the tent repaired in the next village and I was so happy to have my little sanctuary back in working order.

Next day we mounted our trusty bikes and headed north once more. We crossed into Norway and biked along the stunning coastline for a week before boarding a coastal steamship that sails the coast of Norway all year round.

The ship was much like the *Love Boat* and the majority of guests were decidedly better dressed than we were. We were a pair of damp, grubby and slightly smelly cyclists among dry, clean and fresh-scented holidaymakers. We drew a number of stares as we sat down in chairs outside the restaurant and proceeded to prepare our own meal of fish, onions and bread in the same clothes we'd been wearing for five weeks, while other travellers filed into the restaurant in their evening wear!

Even though we were the odd ones out on the boat, I found the cruise absolutely blissful. I didn't have to ride my bike, trudge lengthy tracks or protect myself from mosquitoes. I could just sit and watch the stunning scenery roll past. It was heaven. Even Paul enjoyed the relative luxury for a couple of days.

After disembarking in Norway, we biked over a couple more passes. Finally, after 1904 kilometres on the bike, 600 kilometres by ship and 250 kilometres on foot, we arrived at our most northerly destination, North Cape. Together we rode triumphantly, emerging from the heavy mist hoping to stand at the end of Europe. But it was not to be. Before we got there we were rudely stopped at the gate and asked to pay NZ$25 each to have the privilege of reaching the northernmost point. I couldn't believe it! Indignant and disgusted we turned around and biked back 400 metres and erected our tent. There, within view of the end of the road, we camped near the hallowed ground for free, completely hidden by the mist. It just made me so grateful for the fact that nearly all of New Zealand's significant sites are free for anyone to visit — and long may it stay that way.

Heading south to civilisation, the days were cold and windy with nothing but biking, eating and sleeping. Our route was now cutting across the Norwegian region known as Finnmark. The highlight there was herds of reindeer that roam the area as they have for thousands of year. I was also pretty happy at the lack of mosquitoes. After five days, we arrived in the town of Tromso, the capital of the Troms region of Norway.

In Tromso, Paul stopped in at a camera shop to get something on his camera fixed. We got chatting to the guy in the shop and he was intrigued by our travels. He ended up inviting us to his house for dinner — it was like meeting another Kiwi on the other side of the world. It was great to know that my mum and dad's habit of inviting travellers into their home is not unique — it does happen on the other side of the world!

We had the most delicious meal — the fish soup that his wife cooked for us was one of the best meals I'd had in ages. It was so good to eat something that hadn't come out of cans and been cooked on a camp stove. His wife must have been thinking, 'Oh God, who is he dragging home now?', but we were so grateful to have a home-cooked meal and be in someone's house. The guy just loved meeting people from other cultures and he spent the next couple of days showing us around Tromso and teaching us about life there. We were sad to leave but had to get back on the road.

After another couple of days on our bikes we crossed the border into Finland. My first impression there was people really liked to drink! They were lovely people and they loved their vodka. Once we reached Finland we kept making a trail steadily south doing between 100 and 200 kilometres a day to try and make up the couple of days we'd spent in Tromso. My other impression of Finland was that there are more lakes there than anywhere else I've ever been.

After a train ride and more biking we reached the bottom end of Finland and from there we explored the Aland archipelago that stretches between Finland and Sweden. Returning to Stockholm completed the circle. Stockholm has to be one of the most beautiful cities I've ever been to. There are waterways all over the city and it's clean and easy to navigate. While we were there the water festival was on and the carnival atmosphere was incredible. It was quite a culture shock being back in a city after being out in the wilderness for so long.

After one amazing evening watching fireworks we were making our way back to the camping ground when we saw a girl selling flowers on the side of the road. A drunk guy came past and stole all her flowers. Paul wasn't having a bar of it and grabbed him, telling him to give the flowers back. What he didn't know was that the guy had a whole pile of mates just behind him.

Before we knew it, Paul was being attacked by a group of about twenty angry Yugoslavians. It was terrifying. Paul was on the ground trying to cover his head and I was screaming out for help. When they started sinking their boots into Paul's head, I couldn't think what else to do so I jumped on top of him to try and protect him. My thinking was that they wouldn't kick a girl, but I was wrong. They kicked me in the head before breaking a couple of my fingers and laying into my back. I don't know how long we'd been on the ground before a group of Swedish people came round the corner and broke up the mêlée. The bullies disappeared into the crowd and we slowly picked ourselves up and dragged ourselves back to the camping ground.

Paul was furious. He yelled at me, 'What the fuck were you doing jumping on me like that? I could have dealt with it.' I couldn't do a thing right.

On 11 August we were on our way back home. Our tour up north was over and it was sad that it ended on such a shockingly violent way. I was pretty happy when we got back to Vienna and our little apartment. When I think back on it now, I can barely believe the things I did on that trip. I would never have done any of that stuff on my own so I can thank Paul for motivating me to get out and see the world — even if he could have been a little bit gentler! It was a baptism of fire, but if it hadn't been for him I probably would never have left New Plymouth. It was a big scary world out there and I'd never have been brave enough to go off to London on my own on an OE. It's kind of funny really because that would have been so much easier than touring around Europe with Paul on foot and by bike.

LIFE ON THE DANUBE

You need to paint a picture of the real you

When we got back to Vienna, battered and bruised from our final night in Stockholm, it was time to make some money. We lived like we travelled — as cheaply as possible. As Paul's mother owned our apartment we didn't have to pay rent. That meant that it was really only day-to-day living expenses that we had to find the money for. We discovered one of the best ways to make a bit of money and to be active at the same time was to deliver advertising pamphlets.

In New Zealand, having a pamphlet run is pretty straightforward as most people have their letterboxes out on the street. Not so in Vienna. Paul and I used to ring every doorbell in the apartment buildings until some unsuspecting resident opened the downstairs access door. Then we'd set off on foot up the stairs. A lot of these old buildings didn't have lifts so it wasn't uncommon for us to do ten flights of stairs in each building to deliver junk mail. Once we got inside we'd get abused by any of the residents who saw us. I'd just started to learn German and couldn't speak it very well but I still could tell they weren't happy to see us!

Learning German was quite a mission for me. Paul had taught me some basics of the language while he was recuperating in New Zealand. What little I knew didn't really prepare me for living in Vienna and I set about trying to pick up as much as I could. In the end, I learnt from watching TV and from talking to anyone who had the patience to help me learn.

Vienna itself is a great city to live in. The Danube River, which runs through the city, is beautiful. We used to train on the Danube Trail that ran alongside the river and we'd go up into the vineyards behind the city to run. While Paul was planning the next big trip, he always had to be doing something while we were in Vienna. If we weren't up in the nearby mountains, we were biking a couple of hundred kilometres every weekend or we were working.

There was no such thing as down time. We were always out doing something. I just felt like I was always out of breath and always trying to catch up with Paul.

During my first year in Vienna, I spent a lot of time with Paul's Auntie Fini. She was a traditional Austrian housewife and I used to love going to her house. She taught me how to cook traditional Austrian food all the while patiently teaching me how to speak German. She schooled me in the finer points of being a good Austrian housewife and after about a year I could cook a mean goulash with dumplings followed by vanilla kipfel and I could finally communicate with the people around me.

During the autumn of my first year in Vienna my mother came to stay with us for a couple of months. We were already cramped enough in the flat and Paul was not happy at the thought of her impending visit. I desperately wanted my mum to have a trip overseas and I really wanted her to see where I lived. Although I pointed out to Paul that he'd lived in her house for six months he wasn't having a bar of it. He didn't want anyone to upset our little twosome world.

I couldn't help being excited at the prospect of Mum coming and I didn't really care that Paul wasn't happy about it. He tried explaining that autumn was the most beautiful part of the year and it was the best time to be out on our bikes and he made it clear that I had ruined the autumn for him by inviting my mum to come and stay.

When Mum finally arrived, there was no let-up for me. In the days before she arrived Paul and I had been earning some money by painting his auntie and uncle's house that was about 30 kilometres outside Vienna. Was I going to have a day off because Mum had arrived? Not likely.

I went and met her at the airport and I was excited to see her for the first time in months. We went back to the apartment and dropped off her gear and then I had to get on my bike and cycle out to Fini's house. I couldn't bear leaving Mum at home by herself so we put her on the train to meet us there. When I think back it must have been absolutely awful for her. Here she was, in a foreign country, where people didn't speak much English, just off a series of flights that took more than 24 hours and I put her on a train to God knows where. She must have been terrified.

Still, I wasn't going to argue with Paul about it. As it turned out, Paul had bought her the wrong ticket and a conductor came and tried to fine her 1000 shillings. He even stopped the train while he was trying to make her pay. She didn't know what the hell was going on and ended up getting off the train at the wrong station. Paul should have let me go with her and look after her but trains were only just better than cars in his book so I had to go on my bike.

When we finally arrived at Fini's, she had a huge lunch prepared and she was really excited to meet my mother. The welcome Paul's family gave Mum was great. It was good for me that Mum got to meet the woman who had looked after me so well and taught me German. After lunch, Paul and I went back to work and Mum sat in the garden watching us work. Once we'd finished our work, we all had dinner before heading back into the city. When it came time to go home, I could tell that Mum really didn't want to face getting on the train on her own again. Paul's uncle could see this, too, and said, 'No. Isabel is not going on the train. I'll take her back into town in the car.'

As Paul and I rode back into town, he completely lost his temper. 'That stupid woman can't even catch a train. How hard is that? And now she has to add to the world's pollution by having my uncle make an unnecessary car journey. It's just ridiculous.' I stayed quiet and vowed to take Mum away as much as I could over the next two months so that she didn't have to hear any of Paul's diatribes.

While Mum was over, we took a trip to Hungary. Mum had always had these romantic dreams about going on the Orient Express so we booked tickets to head from Austria across to Budapest. At that time, the Orient Express wasn't the flash train it is now. It was just a normal old train. We had our own compartment on the train but that didn't stop us from getting the odd visitor. At one stage, I went off to the toilet and when I got back to our compartment, there was this incredibly drunk Hungarian bloke accosting Mum. I tore in and grabbed him by the scruff of the neck and chucked him out the door. He wasn't the kind of friendly local you want to meet.

The eastern bloc had just opened up and change was slow in coming to Hungary. When we reached the border, Mum handed her passport over with all her money for the trip folded into the passport. Luckily the guard was an honest one. He just laughed and handed Mum her money back! If he hadn't had such a sense of humour we could have ended up in a Hungarian prison charged with bribery . . .

While we were in Budapest we visited one of the old spas that the city is known for. Mum and I hadn't quite banked on the fact that the Hungarians are quite comfortable going naked at the baths. Thankfully, we were in a female-only part of the baths and we had no choice but to strip off. Leaving the changing room wrapped in our towels, we were chased by a big matronly Hungarian woman who made it abundantly clear that we weren't even allowed to take our towels out to the baths. We did the best to maintain our modesty but we were both freaking out. The woman arrived back shortly carrying a couple of aprons. Apparently you're allowed to wear an apron but not a towel. It wasn't a good look.

When we finally got to the pools we were both really keen to get into the water so we dived into the nearest pool. It was about 40°C and we stayed in there despite the heat because we were too embarrassed to get out! We both absolutely cooked. In the pool with us were about 100 Hungarian ladies who all had plastic hats on to protect their hair. Around the sides of the pool, there were plenty of people getting massage treatments. They were being whacked with bunches of leaves and the noise was incredible. It took us about two hours to get the courage up to get out of the pool again. We must have looked like a pair of crayfish we'd been in the hot water for so long.

Having survived the local baths, Mum and I decided to take an excursion to an amusement park. It was about 150 years old and everything was a bit manky. It looked as if it hadn't been maintained very well during the Communist years and absolutely nothing had been done since independence. We decided to go on this chair-o-plane ride, where you climbed on, belted yourself in and went flying around. In the middle of the ride, the strap that was holding us in broke. We were freaking out. I had visions of being thrown to the ground and killed — thankfully we survived it but it put us both off amusement park rides for a very long time.

In Budapest we stayed at this gorgeous ornate hotel. While it was very beautiful, the service was like something out of *Fawlty Towers*. We had dinner at the hotel one night where we were serenaded by local gypsy musicians. Mum loved the music and kept saying how lovely it was. She smiled away at them and kept saying how lovely it was, not realising that she was meant to be paying them.

The next morning we went down to breakfast only to find that all the leftovers from the previous night had been rehashed and served again. Twice-cooked brussels sprouts wouldn't be my first choice for breakfast. Our waiter then managed to knock over the candle on our table, setting the table cloth on fire. He grabbed the nearest glass of juice and put the flames out managing to spill it over us at the same time.

Mum and I took the opportunity to do some shopping while we were in Budapest and found a great shoe shop. I bought some shoes and decided I liked them so much we went back the next day to buy some more. I wore the shoes that I'd bought the day before and as I left the shop, we were chased down the street by one of the shop assistants who accused me of stealing the shoes. Thankfully I had the receipt with me and could prove that I'd paid for them the previous day.

I was really keen to make sure that Mum saw plenty of Europe while she was staying with me so not long after we got back from Hungary, the pair of us decided to go off to Greece for a couple of weeks. As soon as we had booked to go, Paul announced that he had to go into hospital to have an operation on his foot. Mum and I were so excited to be going off to Greece we went anyway. We thought we were going to have the time of our lives in traditional Greek style. In hindsight, I should have done a bit more research. We ended up spending three weeks in Faliraki in what can only be described as something like an episode of 'Hi-De-Hi!' We were in a really grotty hotel right above a disco. There was nothing but English tourists wanting to drink lager and eat chips. Despite this, we had a great time and it was lovely to be able to relax and act like tourists for a change.

While we were in Faliraki, there was a massive storm and extensive flooding. All the beach deck chairs were washed out to sea and our hotel was full of water. I remember seeing water flowing down the stairs like a waterfall. To make matters worse, we were booked to fly out in the middle of the storm. Sitting on the plane out of Faliraki getting buffeted around and seeing lightning flashing outside was the most scared I've ever been.

When we got back to Vienna, Paul had had his operation. He looked terrible. He'd lost about eight kilos and he complained it was because he couldn't feed himself.

The one nice thing that did happen while Mum was in Vienna was that she got to meet Paul's mother. It turned out that they shared the same birthday. They had been born on the exact same day on opposite sides of the world. Neither of them could speak the other's language but they took an instant liking to each other. We had not long found out that Paul's mother had lung cancer and it was a good distraction for her to meet my mother. She was happy to know that Paul had a nice girlfriend with a nice family who would look after him.

Mum left Vienna in late November, and I was really sad to see her go. I had always been such a home girl before I met Paul and I missed my family like crazy. On the up-side, now that Mum had gone home Paul had me to himself again and he stopped being quite so nasty. And we spent a bit more time with Paul's mother. Apart from the apartment buildings she owned, she also ran a large pharmacy and, despite her failing health and her alcohol dependency, she hated anyone trying to help her. She was a fiercely independent soul and she struggled on her own.

She invited us for Christmas dinner on my first year in Vienna. It was the first time Paul had been inside her home in some years and the sight that met us shocked him to the core. For Christmas lunch she had bought a huge goose, which is a traditional Christmas dish in Austria. Unfortunately, the kitchen was so jam-packed with stuff she couldn't get to the oven. She told us that lunch wasn't quite ready so she sent us out to a local bar for a while. When we got back to the house, the goose was no closer to the oven and she served us some cheese and crackers for lunch. The goose ended up coming home with us and we must have looked pretty funny wandering home with this great big, uncooked bird under our arms.

According to Paul, when he was growing up, his mother had been very prim and proper and expected everything in the house to be just-so. After we got home, he just sat there in complete shock at what had happened to his mother. It was clear then that she was not coping at all and that she needed more help. Just as we realised how bad things were, Paul's mother went downhill really fast. The cancer took hold and it wasn't long before she was completely incapacitated. We knew things had got really bad when one of the people who worked for her at the pharmacy told us they hadn't seen her for three days.

Paul and I went round to her apartment but she wouldn't let us in. We couldn't think of anything else to do so we called the police and they came round and smashed the door down. When we got inside we found his mother lying in her bed. She hadn't been able to move for three days. She was completely dehydrated. It was a terrible thing to see this once proud and beautiful woman reduced to this. She protested all the way to the hospital and said she didn't want to go anywhere. She wanted to die at home. She was not to get her wish and she passed away quietly in the hospital a couple of days later.

Paul was traumatised by it all. Even though he had spent his life trying to run away from her and rebel against her, she was still his mother. He struggled to cope and withdrew deeper into himself.

We were stuck in Vienna for quite a few months. There was just so much to sort out. We had to clean out the apartment and work out exactly what was in there. We found diamond bracelets in ashtrays and gold rings hidden in stacks of towels. We couldn't throw anything out without first checking it because we didn't know what we'd find next.

There was also the question of the pharmacy. Paul and I worked together in the pharmacy trying to clean it out and get it in a fit state for sale. Despite his mother's propensity to work long hours things there were in a bit of a mess. Eventually we got it sorted out and sold it. In the time that we were working together to sort out his mother's estate, Paul and I got on better than we had in ages. He handled what was, for him, a very difficult situation incredibly well and I really got to see more of the good side of him over this time. We worked together well to get everything sorted out over this time.

I spent hours poring over Austrian law to work out just what he was entitled to. It felt like there were sharks circling Paul and I was determined that they weren't going to rip him off. I became quite knowledgeable about tenancy law and found out that the manager of the apartment building that Paul and I lived in had been ripping his mother off for years. We got him fired and got someone honest in the position.

After years of having to scrimp and save and live frugally, Paul was now a wealthy young man. It was a burden that didn't sit easily on him. Until now, I had either been working to look after him or we had been working together. Now things were completely different.

THE RAINS DOWN IN AFRICA

There are no limits except the ones you place

Having been stuck in Vienna for quite a while sorting out Paul's mum's estate, we were both really keen to get away on a trip. Now that he had a bit more money to spend, Paul kitted us both out with new bikes and the best wet-weather gear we could find. We couldn't wait to try out all our new toys.

Paul had spent a bit of time in North Africa and decided he wanted to show me around Tunisia. After a bit of planning, we found ourselves on board a flight to Djerba, a large island off the Tunisian coast. I was so excited to be heading off on a new adventure and I had butterflies in my tummy at the thought of visiting Africa.

When we arrived in Djerba, I was relieved to see our bike boxes waiting for us. Some local kids watched us assemble our bikes — they must have thought we were mad as we biked away from the airport and into the nearby city of Houmt Souk. We dossed down in a cheap hotel and were early to bed to prepare ourselves for biking around this beautiful island.

The next day, as we rode out of Houmt Souk we were surrounded by hundreds of cheeky faced kids who ran alongside our bikes. One of the boys managed to keep up with me on a bike that must have been twice as old as he was!

It had rained heavily over the previous week and the roads were flooded. Paul and I decided to ride on through it and my little friend carried on beside us, leaving the rest of the kids behind at the water's edge. Houses are under water and drains were overflowing. Paul and I soon realised that our planned route might not be passable as many of the unsealed roads we wanted to follow were likely to be flooded. This wasn't a problem we'd reckoned on given that Tunisia is a country known for its lack of water. Eventually, having forded plenty of puddles, we reached the end of the island Djerba and caught the ferry across to the mainland. This provided me with my first look at the Sahara Desert — a stretch of sand that would go on to have a huge influence over my life in years to come.

A long, straight road took us through groves of olive trees and dusty, unkempt villages. By chance we witnessed a near-fatal accident when a child ran in front of an oncoming bus and was all but flattened. Only the quick reactions of the driver prevented a tragedy from occurring. The 3-metre long skid marks on the road showed just how close it had been. The frightened, crying child ran into the arms of his mother and buried his face under the layers of her robes. A little shocked and praising the efforts of the bus driver, we continued on.

On our first night in the desert, we pushed our bikes 400 metres off the road. The air was cold and the sky filled with stars. After so long in Vienna, it was nice to sleep outside in the open air again. The next morning, we got up at 5.15. We were keen to get started as soon as the sun came up. We packed and sat in the cold waiting for the sun to make its appearance — which it finally did at 6.30 am. That was a lesson for us both to stay in our warm sleeping bags and wait for the first warming rays of the sun to appear before racing out onto our bikes.

When we finally got moving it wasn't long before we came across a police patrol checking people's documents. I smiled nervously at the officer as I handed over my New Zealand passport. As I suspected it would, it aroused some interest among the law enforcement officers. Not many people from New Zealand go to that part of the world and even fewer go on bikes. The police officers couldn't believe that we had chosen to travel so far by bicycle. It must have been incomprehensible to them that so-called 'rich' Europeans would choose to cycle when they must surely be able to afford a car.

As soon as Paul had assured them we were married (even though we were only engaged) and that Tunisia was a beautiful country with very friendly people, they let us pass without any problem. We were glad we could go and relieved that we were spared the need to explain our first aid kit, which contained all sorts of vitamins and emergency medication because Paul had heard that misunderstandings over drug abuse in Arab countries can have very unpleasant consequences.

By early afternoon we reached Chenini, a Berber mountain village. A little old Berber woman with a beautifully wrinkled and tattooed face asked us if we wanted to photograph her. We paid the $1.50 she charged, took our shots and she went on her way. Paul was pleased to have the opportunity to take photographs of a local woman. In many parts of the world, particularly in Islamic countries, it is considered rude to take photographs of people, especially women, without first getting their permission.

Below us, in the valley, we could see into the backyards of houses where camels sat in the sunshine and women went about their daily chores. Up by the mosque were a handful of laughing children on a donkey. Before long they spotted us and came running down to beg for pens, sweets and money. I made the mistake of giving one of the kids a small coin and soon my pockets were emptied of all coins. Once we'd run out of things to give the kids we knew it was time to leave.

Our next stage lead us through the mountains of Dahar on a track whose condition left a lot to be desired. As we climbed, I started having trouble with my left knee, which I'd overstrained. We'd left Vienna in winter and I was now bearing the consequences of not having trained sufficiently before setting off on this trip. But I carried on, pedalling with one leg, which was a difficult task on a hill track with a fully loaded bike. We crawled along at walking speed for the rest of the day. Time and again I had to dismount and push while Paul waited for me.

'At this speed we'll never get out of here,' I moaned. I knew we had to cover more than 100 kilometres of piste before reaching the next village.

Just before nightfall, I heard a pop and pheeeewww. My tyre had blown. Paul fixed it hastily while I tried to find a good place to camp. Not far on, we found an olive plantation, which we figured would provide us with some shelter overnight. Meanwhile the sky darkened and the wind started to rustle in the trees. I was in bed by 8 pm, trying to keep my knee as straight as possible in the hope that it would recover a bit overnight.

At about three in the morning, I was woken as sand blew into my mouth. Outside it was blowing a gale and fine grains of sand had managed to find their way into our tent — not a good sign for the next day's ride.

When I next woke, the wind had calmed down and my knee felt better so we carried on slowly up the mountain pass. Soon we came to a fork in the track and the view ahead commanded our respect. A sea of desert hills that all look confusingly similar stretched out as far as the horizon. At the risk of getting hopelessly lost, we had to decide which path to take. We had only two and a half litres of water left and could easily get lost if the track continued to split like this.

We decided to carry on until four that afternoon and we marked the path with stones as we went. That way we knew that if we hadn't found the next town by four, we could turn around and follow our tracks back to the fork. It took us five hours of hard going before we found a rusted old sign with hand-painted writing — Toujane. At last, confirmation that we'd taken the right track. Two hours later, we arrived at our long awaited destination, Matmata, where some of the original *Star Wars* movies had been filmed. That fact still draws heaps of visitors to Matmata today.

As soon as we were alone, I searched for a hidden spot in which to answer an urgent call of nature. This is a very difficult undertaking in a country where foreigners are of such interest that, at any time, someone will pop out of nowhere and disturb your most private moment. I got off my bike, ran up a bank then jumped down the other side. Not the smartest thing as I landed with my head one foot away from the power line. Even though I'd come perilously close to electrocution, I still needed to go to the toilet so I hastily dealt with business before heading back to the safety of the road.

On the following morning we tackled our next trail with no real difficulties. By lunchtime, we'd arrived at a town called El Hamma. Even though we'd had a cruisy morning, it wasn't long before all hell broke loose. At the entrance to the village a group of 30 or 40 children and teenagers were playing soccer. One of them saw us and yelled, 'TOURIST!' They all dropped what they were doing and stormed towards us.

'Uh oh, we're in for trouble, just speed up a bit,' yelled Paul. Some of the kids blocked the road yelling at us to stop. Others gathered stones for the attack. I pulled my sunglasses down and tried to look determined as I cycled through the mob. Most of them jumped out of my way at the last second but a couple of them decided to run after me. Thankfully we managed to get away unscathed despite the hail of stones that followed us. But it wasn't over. All the way into town we ran a gauntlet of stone throwers, spitting, yelling and laughter. It was an unnerving welcome.

In the centre of town things were quieter so we stopped to stock up with supplies. As soon as we had dismounted we were surrounded by kids. Thank goodness they were friendly — all smiles and laughter. Still, we left town as fast as we could, glad to be alone again.

For the first time on tour we had a strong tail wind that sent us flying at 30 kilometres an hour over the straights towards the beginning of the sand desert. In a town called Douz we hired a guide for a two-day camel trek into the dunes. Our guide, Yousef, was soon nicknamed Joe. He introduced us to our camels, Mitsi and Wobbly. I squealed with a mixture of fright and delight as Mitsi stood up. I clung tightly to Mitsi's saddle for the first few minutes until I got used to her long, rolling, stride. Joe led us out into the dunes pulling the camels along behind him while we enjoyed the ride and view.

Despite the scenery, what caught most of my attention were the camels. They were such comical creatures that make rude noises, have bad breath, dribble a lot and who, when mistreated, can take revenge on their owners. Paul told me he'd heard of camels that killed their owners by sitting on them in the middle of the night. At the end of our ride through the dunes Joe tied the front legs of each camel together to make sure they didn't go wandering off in the night. I hoped they wouldn't avenge themselves on us for that! I didn't fancy Mitsi's heavy backside squashing the wind out of me in the night!

Joe prepared two fires to cook our evening meal of ragout and flat bread. The bread was prepared from flour, water and salt and kneaded into a large, round shape that was laid in the ashes of one fire and covered. Meanwhile our ragout was cooking in a big pot. After two hours our meal was ready. To Joe's delight we all ate in the traditional Tunisian manner, out of the same pot, dipping the still-warm bread in the stew. It was — and still is — one of the best meals I've ever eaten.

As the fire died down, the cold crept in and we retired to our hand-woven woollen blankets for the night. Next morning Joe had the fire going before the sun was up and the bread-making ritual was repeated before the camel's legs were released and we were on our way back.

Our next stop was El Faouar, an unexciting little village that marked the end of human habitation at the edge of the desert. Paul had promised me that we'd check into a hotel here and I couldn't wait. Since our arrival in Tunisia I hadn't even been able to wash my hands properly, let alone the rest of me, due to the severe water shortage.

When we arrived in El Faouar, we followed the sign that said 'hotel' and we were surprised to find a very grand three-star hotel in this poor looking village. We were even more surprised to find that a room would cost us 36 dinars — about NZ$50 — a fortune by Tunisian standards. I was really disappointed although we agreed that it was way too much for our budget. As we turned to leave, the man on reception took pity on us and offered us a room for just 20 dinars. How could we refuse?

After a blissful hot shower, Paul and I went wandering in the dunes. I felt a bit guilty for having enjoyed the luxury of hot water and a nicely decorated room while all the local people drew their water from wells and had very basic houses. The people were glad to earn money any way they could and even the children didn't let an opportunity pass. From over a kilometre away three kids had recognised us as tourists and had come scrambling over as fast as they could, one carried a sand rose, a stone from the Sahara, and another a baby desert fox with whom he posed for photographs.

The poor wee animal tried constantly to escape and the fear in his eyes said everything about the torture he was going through. I wanted to buy his freedom but he would have died out in the desert alone. With a heavy heart and lighter pockets we continued on our way.

Back at the hotel it was dinner time and a beautiful buffet was set out before us. After weeks of living on whatever food we could buy out in the countryside, I was excited at the prospect of a proper meal. With eyes as big as dinner plates, I rather too enthusiastically shovelled the food into my mouth. Uh-oh, what was that? A whole chilli pepper burned its way down my throat and into my stomach. I felt like there was steam pouring out my ears. The drinks in the restaurant were way too expensive for our tight budget and even in pain, I knew that drinking local water wasn't going to help things at all so I just had to try and breathe through the heat.

Paul laughed as I desperately coughed and spluttered trying to get rid of the intense chilli heat. I tried to keep on eating as I'd been so excited at the prospect of a good meal but my appetite had been well and truly scorched.

In the morning, I awoke to the sight of Paul coming out of the bathroom gagging. During the night it had rained and the sewerage system hadn't coped with the extra water. As a result, the hotel pipes had backed up and the smell wafting up made this strong man weak at the knees. Needless to say we vacated our room early.

Our plan for the day had been to ride over a sand trail that was marked on our map. When we got to where the trail was supposed to start we found that it didn't exist. We were left with two choices, either bike or take a bus back over the 70 kilometres we'd ridden to get to El Faouar. We opted for the second choice and were pleasantly surprised at the bus driver's willingness to stick us, bikes and all, on board. The only problem was that the bus that left El Faouar almost empty filled with more and more people at each stop along the way. Before long, we could hardly breathe for the people, goats, chickens and goods jammed in around us.

After one and a half hours packed in like sardines, we finally arrived in Kebili, where we hopped off the bus and back onto our bikes. We then headed north to cross Chott El Djerid, a 7000-square-kilometre salt lake, the largest of its kind in the Sahara. As we made our way across the lake, the wind blew ever stronger in our faces and the kilometres were slow to pass. The road was long, flat and straight, giving me plenty of time to digest some of the experiences, sights, smells and images of the lake.

After 20 kilometres of flat sand, we arrived at the start of the salt crystals and a landscape I could never have imagined — a flat sea of dried salt crystals, resembling ice, stretched as far as the eye could see. It was how I imagined Antarctica would look, which was pretty strange in the middle of the sandy Sahara.

We rode all day and in the evening we still found ourselves far from solid ground so we decided to camp on the salt lake not far from a wrecked bus that had been abandoned after it had sunk into the salt crust. Even though the salt looked quite solid, parts of it were like quicksand that you could disappear into, never to be seen again. Aside from this, many people had lost their lives in this place suffering from lack of water and overcome by heat, but that was during the summer months.

Even though the area only gets about 100 millimetres of rain each year, we were worried that some of it was going to fall overnight. A part of the lake already stood underwater and we didn't want to wake to find that we were, too.

We pushed our bikes about a kilometre off the road and set up camp. The atmosphere was unique and the sunset unbelievably beautiful. I could hardly believe that less than 24 hours ago I was wandering in the sand dunes of the Sahara and now I was sitting in a landscape that resembled the Antarctic. The extremes of this land impressed me.

In the morning we were up early and were surprised to find that, although it hadn't rained, the ground water levels had risen overnight and the water was slowly flowing across the crust of salt. The edge of the water was now only 150 metres away from our tent. Just as well we'd decided to get up to photograph the sunrise or we could have been swimming back to the road.

After we left the salt lake, we headed for the start of the Djebel en-Negeb mountains on the border with Algeria. We had been told to expect stringent military controls but were pleasantly surprised when we were waved through. They must have felt sure that terrorists wouldn't be travelling by bicycle.

The atmosphere in this part of the country was different as it is so isolated. Whenever we rode into an oasis I felt like an actor in a Wild West movie heading for the last frontier. The oases were dirty and desolate, many buildings only half built. Groups of men lay around in doorways and on the ground, draped in blankets playing dominos, smoking water pipes and chatting.

In one village we visited a restaurant. It was just a dirty concrete shelter with plastic chairs. With dirty knives and forks we ate a surprisingly tasty meal trying not to think about what it might have been. We ordered seconds, and would have devoured a third course if we hadn't been too embarrassed to ask. We washed our meal down with Coke, to avoid the water as an insurance against the dreaded dysentery common in such countries, and carried on our way.

Eventually we made our way back to Djerba to catch our flight back to Vienna. My first experience of the Sahara had been one of impressive landscapes, and exotic, interesting and friendly people — for the most part! I had enjoyed the excitement of discovering a new land and culture with a rich history, new-to-me religion and interesting traditions. It had given me a chance to view the world from a different perspective and had opened my mind and broadened my attitudes to encompass a different way of life. Even though I'd travelled extensively in Europe, this was the first time that I had been immersed in a culture completely different from Western society and I loved it.

Transporting bikes

Some airlines will carry bicycles free of charge but it is always advisable to book your bicycle in when you purchase your ticket and to limit your total luggage to no more than 25 kilograms.

Each airline has their own packing requirements but it is usually sufficient when the pedals are removed, the handle bars are turned and the air from the tyres released.

When possible it is advisable to pack the bicycle in a bike box available from most cycle shops. This protects the bike from damage and avoids any problems with difficult airline employees who may want to make life hard for you.

INTO THE DESERT

What others think of you can have no effect unless you let it

After my experience in Tunisia, the prospect of a trek in the desert in
Egypt was very appealing. In 1996, Paul had done a reconnaissance
trip with another adventurer called Alvis. A survival expert from
Yugoslavia, Alvis took groups on desert adventure tours for a living.
He and Paul did a walking trek through the Arabian Desert in Egypt
trying to work out whether it would be possible to take commercial
guided trips through the area. Paul had absolutely loved the Arabian
Desert and was dead keen for me to experience this bleak and beautiful
part of the world the way he had. When Alvis decided to put together
a group to do the trek the following year, Paul encouraged me to take
part without him. He couldn't have known then that it would cause
the life that he'd created for the pair of us to completely unravel.

I flew into Hurghada and met up with the rest of the group.
I was a bit nervous to be going off on a trek with people I didn't

know but it didn't take long before I was comfortable being around everyone else. There were twelve of us, all from Austria, but from different backgrounds and with varying levels of ability. We spent nine days crossing Egypt between the Nile River and the Red Sea. It was 150 kilometres and it was pretty easy compared to what I'd been expecting. There were plenty of rest periods and places along the way to get water.

It was a real eye-opener for me. For the first time, I was out in the wilderness without Paul and, more importantly, I was with other people away from the pressure that Paul constantly put on me. We'd spent nearly every moment together since we'd met and over that time I didn't really have any other friends. It was unusual of him to want me to go on a trip on my own but he really wanted me to experience what he'd seen in the Arabian Desert.

I'd had three years of being told how hopeless, how unco and how unfit I was. Compared to Paul, I was all those things, or so I believed it. Being in the desert was a total revelation to me. The people in our group all seemed pretty fit, adventurous and sporty but I was running circles around them all.

At night, when we'd stopped to rest they'd all be absolutely shattered from the heat, the sand and the exertion. Not me. I'd be off up the nearest hill to check out the view or I'd go for a run just to burn off my excess energy. Even though the nights were cold and my sleeping bag was thin so I didn't sleep well, I just loved being in the desert and I loved the challenge of being away from civilisation. Compared to being on trips with Paul, this was a piece of cake.

For the first time in years, someone told me I was amazing and capable. On top of that, I'd actually made friends with people other than Paul. These people liked me for me and they were impressed with my abilities. I felt on top of the world. My confidence, which had been so badly eroded over the past few years, started to sneak back.

While I was in Egypt walking through the Arabian Desert, Paul was making his final preparations to carry out an altogether more dangerous mission with Alvis and another bloke, Gunther. Once we came out of the Arabian Desert, the four of them were going to cross the Libyan Desert in southern Egypt. It was going to be a 10-day, 250-kilometre unsupported trek through a closed military zone. Everything they needed for the trip they'd have to take with them, including all of their food and water. There had never been any mention of me going and I really didn't think that I'd be fit enough or fast enough to go with them. That all changed while we were in the Arabian Desert. Alvis was so impressed with my ability that he invited me to join them on the Libyan Desert trek. I was totally unprepared to do the trek but I was so stoked that someone thought I was good enough I agreed to do it.

I knew I didn't have the right gear for the Libyan Desert so I set about buying what I could off my mates on the Arabian Desert trip. I bought a really warm but really heavy sleeping bag off one of them. It weighed more than three kilos but it was worth lugging that extra weight to make sure I'd be warm on the cold desert nights to come.

To cross the Arabian Desert I'd only taken a pair of running shoes. I knew that these wouldn't be enough on our next trek so I managed to borrow a pair of tramping boots off another member of the party — only they were half a size too small. I had no money and I thought they'd do.

I thought that Paul would be happy for me that Alvis thought I was up to the adventure. And he was — for a while. Until he realised that he'd have to bring food and provisions for both of us and not just for him. Once again, everything was all about Paul. But I didn't care. Alvis and I flew from Hurghada back to Cairo on the verge of one of the biggest adventures of my life.

OFF THE GRID IN EGYPT — THE LIBYAN DESERT

Push yourself to your limits and see for yourself what you are capable of becoming

Speaking Arabic and knowing Cairo like the back of his hand, Alvis had booked us into a hotel in one of the less affluent parts of the city. Well, I say hotel, actually it was a filthy old brothel. But it was cheap and that's what mattered. Even though I hadn't had a shower for a week and hadn't slept in a bed in the same amount of time, I was still bloody thankful that we only had to spend one night there.

Paul and Gunther were due to arrive at Cairo airport at nine that night. I remember sitting in the smelly room looking at my backpack going through the maths. Adding the figures over and over again — 20 litres of water, 3.3 kilograms of sleeping bag, 2 kilograms of food. No matter how I added it the result came to a heavy 35 kilograms. Could I walk across the desert with that on my back?

It was only a day since I finished my trek across the Arabian Desert. My legs were sore and I was exhausted. Not exactly in prime condition to tackle a long and dangerous trip. Eventually, Alvis and I went out into the streets of Cairo to get more provisions before heading for the airport. It was Ramadan in Cairo and, after nightfall, the city really came alive. The streets were chaotic with people and sounds and smells. It was a shock to my system after nine days of peace in the desert.

The poorest of the population were seated on the footpath in rows waiting for a free evening meal. Smiling children with big eyes and plastic plates waited excitedly, women with their heads shrouded in cloth sat patiently. Plates of flat bread and stew were being prepared en masse. Time and time again we were invited to join in the meal with the locals but Alvis and I had water to buy and a plane to meet so we just smiled and walked on.

Buying water to last four of us our whole trek was not an easy feat. Somehow we managed to find and purchase 45 litres of safe bottled water in a part of the city where locals drank straight from the tap. Every shop we went into, Alvis got the same reaction from the shopkeepers. 'Forty-five litres?' They must have thought we were crazy but after two hours we had our water ration, which we dropped off back at the 'hotel'.

Before heading out to the airport, I packed my bag. Every single unnecessary piece was thrown out and 20 one-litre bottles of water went in, stacked in two layers. I went to try and lift my pack onto my back and Alvis caught it. 'Stop,' he growled. 'No one is allowed to lift their own pack, we can't afford a back injury in the desert.' Suits me, I thought, I couldn't lift it anyway. He helped me to put my pack on. And all I could think was, 'Oh shit! You've got to be kidding. How the hell am I going to walk 250 kilometres across the desert with this on my back? I'm not even sure I can walk across the room.'

Having come this far there was no way I was going to back out now. Thankfully, Alvis saw that I was struggling and made some adjustments to the position of the pack leaving it sitting firmly on my hips instead of on my back. The difference it made was huge. Maybe, just maybe, I could do this after all.

By 9 pm we were out at the airport waiting for Paul and Gunther to arrive from Vienna. Well, we were at the airport but at the wrong terminal. The taxi that we'd caught out there 'wasn't authorised to deliver us to the other terminal'. Yeah, right. There was no way we were going to bribe the guy so Alvis and I ended up running what seemed about 3 kilometres to the other terminal, hoping like hell the plane would be late.

You should always be careful what you wish for. The plane was late. Seven hours late. To make matters worse, as we weren't arriving or departing we weren't allowed to stay in the terminal building. It was freezing cold outside, but there was nothing for it — we had to wait out there with everybody else.

The plane finally arrived at four in the morning, just three hours before we were due to be on a bus to Farafra, our starting point. I ran to hug Paul. Straight away it was clear he wasn't happy. He hissed at me, 'How dare you hug me, we're in a Muslim country'. It didn't matter to him that this was an airport and all around us people were hugging and kissing, happy to see each other.

Things quickly went from bad to worse. Paul reckoned he hadn't been able to take enough water on the plane because he'd had to carry provisions for me. As a result he'd got dehydrated and now he had a cold. It was *all* my fault. He was in a stinking mood and there was nothing I could do about it. It hadn't occurred to me that Paul would feel threatened but, clearly, he did. This was the first time we'd ever done an expedition with other people — much less with someone else leading the expedition. It was clear that the next few days were not going to be easy. When we got back to the brothel we had a quick briefing to make sure everything was in order. It was so late there was nothing much we could have done anyway. We left with just enough time to get to the bus station.

The ride south — nine hours in an old dunger of a bus on bumpy, dusty roads — took us deep into the Sahara. Having hardly slept in the past three days I tried to catch some shuteye but I was overtired and hyped — a lethal combination. Scarcely a word was said among our team the whole trip. We all knew the plan and talking about what we were about to do wasn't going to help anything.

We arrived in Farafra at about four in the afternoon. This is the last town on the edge of a closed military zone that stretches south all the way to the Libyan border. We had to disappear into the desert unseen. We had no permits and there was no way we'd be able to talk ourselves out of it if we were caught. We'd be jailed as spies because we were carrying satellite pictures of the area and a primitive GPS navigation system. There were no accurate maps of the area so that's all we had to work with. I didn't dare to think about the consequences of such a scenario for me as a Western woman in an Islamic, Arabic country.

We had to wait until night fell before we could really make our way into the desert. Until then we just had to pretend to be tourists taking a walk on the outskirts of the town. By about six o'clock the sun started to go down and we prepared ourselves to really get moving. At this point, we thought our trip was over before it had started when three local men approached us to find out what we were doing. Alvis managed to convince them that we were just having a picnic and watching the sunset. They seemed happy with his explanation and they went on their way.

As every minute passed, the anticipation rose in me. I knew I should have been scared out of my wits but I was so focused on what was ahead of me that I was impatient for the sun to set and for us to get going. When the sun finally dropped over the horizon, we were off. Gunther and Paul helped me put on my pack with its 20 litres of water. We were going to try to do the whole trek in seven days but in case it took us longer — we'd allowed 10 days — we were rationed to 2 litres of water each a day. It might sound like quite a lot but when you're trekking through a desert, climbing hills and tackling sandstorms, believe me, it's not.

Alvis had been planning this trek for two years. He was undoubtedly the leader of the expedition and, as such, he had responsibility for navigation and also for keeping us all together and keeping us safe. It was pretty clear from the outset that Paul didn't like having someone else tell him what to do. I don't know if he'd have been the same if I wasn't there — maybe it was just a macho thing, I'm not sure.

When we finally left the oasis and headed into the desert, it was at a fast pace. Within an hour we'd put 7 kilometres between us and town without being spotted. It was pitch black and I found myself struggling through deep sand. The terrain was quite bumpy and I couldn't see my feet.

The reason for the bumps in the sand soon became obvious. Alvis told us all to stop and change direction. The bumps were vehicle tracks in the sand and we'd spent the past hour criss-crossing an area near a military base to try to make it hard for us to be followed. The possibility of getting caught out here suddenly became very real for me. My heart was pumping so fast that I wouldn't have been surprised if the others could hear it.

In order to make sure we were a long way from the military we walked pretty much all night. At around midnight we stopped for a brief rest but the cold soon started to seep in and we knew we had to keep moving. The darkness was so all encompassing that I'm glad I wasn't in charge of navigation.

By four in the morning, the temperature had dropped to about −3 degrees. It's one of the most surprising things about being in the desert — no matter how hot it is during the day, at night the temperature can drop dramatically. You really have to be prepared for extreme temperature change.

The sun finally started to make its way into the sky at about six in the morning. I was so relieved to be able to see where I was walking and also to take in the beauty of the desert. Ahead in the distance stood a range of mountains and closer still there was a series of table-topped hills. The landscape was mind blowing — golden sand, white limestone all in sharp contrast against a clear blue sky. We decided to dump our gear for a little while and climb to the top of one of the hills. It was such a relief to get my pack off my back and to be able to walk to the top of the hill. The slopes were steep and crumbly so it was pretty hard going but the view made it all worthwhile. And, for once, we felt quite safe because we could have seen anyone coming or any military installations for miles in all directions.

We decided that this would be a good time to rest. It wasn't perhaps the smartest choice as this was the coolest part of the day but Alvis and I were both in desperate need of sleep. Paul was not happy. He thought that we should carry on while it was still cool. As the photographer on the trip, Paul took this time to go and take some photographs of the surrounding landscape. We had agreed that if he wanted to take photos he would have to do it during our rest stops as we didn't want to have to stop walking so he could take pictures. If he did take photos while we were walking, he knew that we'd keep going and he'd have to catch up. Being the photographer meant that Paul was carrying 8 kilograms more gear than the rest of us.

On this particular rest break all I wanted to do was sleep. But Paul had other ideas. He thought that I should be helping him carry camera gear and set up shots. I was clearly struggling and my feet were a mess. While the too-small tramping boots had seemed OK in Cairo, my feet and legs had swollen up and they were now causing me all sorts of pain. I spent some time tending to my feet, applying plasters and trying to clean the blisters.

After sorting out my feet I had a few sips of precious water before settling down to sleep. Paul wanted me to go with him on a photography mission but Alvis intervened, 'Can't you see she needs to rest? She can't do that. She's already at her limits!' I tried to help him but I couldn't get up so in the end Paul went off on his own, quietly fuming at having been over-ruled by Alvis.

Three hours later, I awoke to hear Paul putting his gear back in his pack. The sun was absolutely scorching and I knew it was time to get moving again. The combination of the heat, the soft sand and the lack of water made it incredibly tough to keep moving. The guys had got well into their water supplies but I had worked out that if I drank as little as possible during the day when I was hot and drank my ration of water at night, my cells would take up the water more readily instead of sweating it straight out again. During the day I drank only enough to wet my mouth. After a while the torturous thirst all but disappeared by the evening when I would allow myself to drink.

By two o'clock in the afternoon we came across a small limestone formation. It was one of the few things in the desert that threw a shadow. We huddled into the shade that the small shadow offered us and took the chance to rest. Up ahead in the distance we saw a caravan consisting of a woman, six camels and a donkey. It was a magical sight and it made me feel as if I was on a film set. Everything seemed so unreal and beautiful — well, everything except my feet that is. There was nothing beautiful or unreal about the pain they were causing me.

We stayed there for a few hours until the sun started to lose its fierceness. We'd decided to walk on in darkness so as not to lose any more precious water. By the time the sun set completely we'd established a good rhythm and we were all prepared to carry on into the night. Paul decided to go off and take some photographs as the sunset was particularly beautiful. Alvis told him that if he wanted to take photos he would have to catch up with the rest of us as he wasn't prepared for us all to wait for him. One of the key things about these kinds of trips is that once you get your rhythm or you're in the zone, you should keep going. It's really hard to get into that kind of phase and stopping for someone else to do something is really difficult.

Paul went off with his camera, his tripod and a couple of lenses. He expected me to go after him but I wasn't prepared to stop walking to help him. Alvis, Gunther and I carried on and expected Paul would catch up in a few minutes. Once 10 minutes had passed though I started to worry. The lower the sun got, the more I worried. What if something had happened to Paul? What if he'd fallen? What if he'd got lost? So many questions ran through my mind. With every passing minute the sky got darker. Alvis realised that I was starting to stress but he said nothing. Eventually, he turned round and scanned the way we had come in the hope of spotting Paul. 'He knows the rules. He'll catch up,' was all he said. That was cold comfort to me. 'But what if he misses us in the dark and loses our tracks?'

Alvis hesitated a moment, looked up ahead and said 'Damn. We'll have to camp up here for the night.' He was angry. Stopping for the whole night because of Paul's stubbornness would put us all behind. It would mean we'd have to walk further in the sun tomorrow and it would mean that we'd lose precious water rations.

I could tell that if Paul did make it back to us, the tension that had been in the air since his arrival at the airport was going to explode and that would mean big problems for everyone. It seemed whatever happened, it was going to be dramatic. Ten minutes after we'd stopped to make camp, Paul caught us up.

Alvis was furious. 'We're staying here for the night. We couldn't risk losing you and now our schedule is all messed up.' Paul hated Alvis talking to him like this. And even more he hated that Alvis had doubted his ability for even a moment. 'I was perfectly capable of catching up,' he snapped.

'I didn't know that,' replied Alvis. 'And anyway Lisa was getting very worried.' I was torn by the whole exchange. Paul was my partner and I knew I should have been backing him up but he'd hardly spoken to me since we met at the airport. Besides, I knew how precarious things were on this trip. He might have had the confidence that he could finish this trip, but I certainly didn't.

While these two male egos squared off against each other, Gunther said nothing. He was the quiet, easy-going, easy-to-please member of the expedition. He took no sides and went about his business undisturbed. For his calming presence I was truly grateful. I couldn't imagine what it would have been like if all three of them had got involved in this 'discussion'.

Paul and Alvis continued arguing for about an hour until Paul turned his attention on to me. Then it all came out. It was my fault that he had got a cold. It was my fault he hadn't been able to get more water to bring. It was my fault that we hadn't had a proper brief before we left Cairo.

I was angry at Paul as I knew that the only hope we had of surviving to the end of our journey was to retain some sense of harmony and cooperation within the group. I decided that the only way I was going to survive the days ahead was to shut myself off and to concentrate on what I had to do to get out in one piece.

We stayed in that camp until about three in the morning. The air of tension that hung over us all made it difficult to sleep. When I heard Alvis packing his gear, I knew I had to get up and get moving. My bones were tired. My feet were in a shocking state and you could have cut the air with a knife — not exactly an ideal situation. It was another one of those moments where I longed to be snuggled up in bed at my parents' house in Oakura.

Thank goodness they didn't know where I was. Mum would have worried herself sick. She knew that I'd been in the Arabian Desert the previous week but back then phone calls were really expensive. I'd only ring home once every few months — and the cheapest way of communicating was by letter. While I was in Cairo I'd taken the time to write Mum and Dad a letter telling them where I was going and what I was planning to do. I told them I loved them and that if they hadn't heard from me by the time they got the letter, then something had probably gone wrong. Thankfully, by the time they got the letter, they already knew I was OK!

We started off in the dark again and my eyes longed for sunlight and the warmth of the sun's first rays. As the day finally started to dawn we found ourselves in the most magical place — a kind of mini Grand Canyon stood before us, only the colours were different. Instead of reds everything was pink and white in the early morning sun. We were all completely blown away by the beauty of the scene. So much so that Alvis even agreed to stop for an hour so we could take it in and Paul could photograph the changing light in the canyon.

Up until this point, we'd managed to cover the required 45 kilometres per day that would see us complete the trip within the allotted 10 days. But ahead of us were the mountains that we'd seen in the distance the day before. There was no obvious path over them — although if there had been we probably wouldn't have used it because of the risk of being caught. Alvis studied the satellite pictures and decided that the best way forward was to climb up to the nearest plateau and hope for the best. The scale of these pictures was 1:500,000 so everything we did was a gamble — an informed one but a gamble nonetheless.

Slowly we picked our way up the steep slopes. The rock was loose and would give way underfoot. It would have been a hard climb without a huge pack but carrying a load that was two-thirds of my body weight made it extremely difficult and energy sapping. When we got to the top of the first plateau, we were disappointed. From there we could see that instead of being one table-top plateau, what we were going to have to get over was a seemingly unending series of mountains and valleys. We were going to have to continually climb up and down until we came to the other side, which we couldn't see.

By the time we'd climbed a few of these peaks, the sun really started to burn and I knew that it wasn't just me suffering. Eventually we took refuge in a spot of shade provided by a rocky outcrop. It wasn't long, though, before the sun had chased this shadow away and we were left looking for another place to hide from its burning rays.

A couple of hundred metres away was another spot of shade. We just left our gear where it was and headed to the next refuge. There we sat talking about the most important thing in our world — water.

It turned out that Paul and Alvis only had half a litre left of their daily ration. Gunther had slightly more at three quarters of a litre. Me, I still had one and a half litres due to my strict policy of not drinking it in the heat of the day. At that point, it became clear to me that the three of them would not be able to make it through the desert on just two litres a day. Paul was suffering worst because his cold was constantly drying his mouth out. He'd been drinking three litres of water a day and, at that rate, would have to finish the trek in seven days.

Alvis and Gunther were also drinking more than their allotted share, both getting through two and a half litres a day. From this point on, I decided, I'd have to try and survive on one and a half litres a day in case one of the others got in trouble. We'd have to make sure we kept going at a good pace if we were going to get out of there.

Paul suddenly declared that he felt unsafe being separated from his water supply and he headed back to where we'd left our packs.

The rest of us followed him down to where the gear was and agreed to get on our way. The rest of the day was pure frustration. We seemed to be going up and down mountains with no end in sight.

No sooner would we summit one but there would be another one in our way. Just before sunset, we found ourselves on the edge of a cliff looking out over yet another valley and another mountain. It was getting dark but we still managed to pick our way down into that valley safely but slowly.

By the time we made camp, it was nine o'clock. We'd been going since 3.30 in the morning and we had only covered 16 kilometres. That was less than half our daily target. We all agreed that tomorrow would be a big day as we needed to make up some of that deficit.

I knew that there was no way I could cover the required 45 or more kilometres that the following day would ask of me if I didn't lose some weight. And given that I was only about 50 kilos, it was going to be my pack that the weight came out of. Out went half of my food. I'd hardly been able to eat any of it anyway so it wouldn't be a great loss. This was in the days before freeze-dried meals and high-energy supplements. I jettisoned some stale bread and a block of cheese. All I kept was chocolate and some dried fruit. I would just have to live on scroggin for the next few days.

The next morning, as we reached the top of the very last mountain, we found ourselves in a different world. Here there was sand, sand and more sand. After crossing all those mountains we faced another problem — sandhills. The sand was unbelievably deep and it got in our boots, in our clothes and packs. It was incredibly beautiful but it offered no shade. It was that picture-book view of the Sahara — golden, vast and, well, sandy.

My boots soon filled with sand and it caused real problems with my feet. At one of our rest stops during the day, I took my boots off to check out just how bad things were. My feet were an absolute mess. My right foot felt like it was just one big blister and the pain was excruciating. With every day the blisters were getting worse but there was nothing I could do about it except to carry on.

The first 10 minutes after each rest stop were the worst as I had to really force myself to move. This is one landscape that humans can only survive in if they're moving. If you stop for too long, your water will run out and then your time is up. The damage to my feet was shocking but not enough to make me lose the will to live. I had to keep moving.

By noon we were all melting. There was no shade anywhere and in the end we gave up searching and just lay down in the sand. The temperature was above 45°C and the cheap sunscreen I'd brought with me was no match for the burning sun. My tongue was sticky and swollen. My lips were cracked and dry. I couldn't swallow even if I'd wanted to have a drink of water. With our last remaining reserves of energy the four of us managed to dig a hole in the ground to lie in. The sand underneath us was cool and I managed to hang my sleeping mat over the hole to provide us with some much needed shade.

'One hour,' said Alvis, 'and then we'll search for some more shade.'

The hour was soon up and we got back on our feet and carried on searching for the lithest of shadows to rest in. One hour. Nothing. Two hours. Nothing. Eventually we just collapsed in the sand again. We'd all lost too much moisture and were more exhausted than ever. The heat was unbearable, relentless.

Since the argument two days before, Paul had become more and more withdrawn. He was angry at me for, well, pretty much everything. And he was angry at Alvis for contradicting him in front of me. He was clearly also suffering badly from lack of water. I had neither the energy nor the will to argue with him.

Lying there, collapsed in the sand, things took a surreal turn. Paul asked Alvis if he could speak to him alone. They went off a few metres away and I could tell that the discussion was pretty fiery. When they came back to where Gunther and I were resting, Alvis told us the news that I realised I had almost been expecting. Paul had decided to continue the trip on his own.

A range of emotions washed over me. I was devastated that Paul could bring me out into the desert and then just leave me here. I had to focus on surviving. I was frightened that he wouldn't make it through alive. Even though I knew that he was more than capable of doing the rest of the trip on his own, I also knew that one wrong step out there could be your last.

More than all of these emotions, I was angry — angry at myself for having decided to come and angry at Paul for leaving me there. I lay in the middle of a burning desert, miles from anywhere with scarcely any provisions and hardly any water. Precious water rolled down my cheeks and I felt what little energy I had drain out of my body. Paul came over and tried to comfort me.

At that moment I knew that my relationship with Paul was over. Never again would he make me feel so bad about myself. He'd dominated my life for long enough. I needed to live my own life. I needed freedom.

Paul returned to where Gunther and Alvis were sitting. I stayed put, took a deep breath and gathered all my strength. For the first time in ages, I had to think for myself. I heard Paul tell Alvis to look after me. With this thought in my mind I felt my determination return.

Paul prepared himself to go and tried to console me. The tears that had come to me moments ago had stopped. I knew I couldn't afford to cry as it was just a waste of water. Paul's last words to me were, 'It'll be all right'. Then he hugged me and disappeared over the sandhills. Again, I felt like I was in a movie, it was completely surreal. With every step that he took away from me, I separated myself and my energy from him. I hoped he would be all right but I would go on. I wouldn't waste my precious reserves worrying about him, now I had to take care of myself.

As soon as Paul was out of sight, Alvis turned to me. I could tell he didn't quite know what to say or do. He was probably thinking he'd now have a hysterical woman on board for the rest of the trip. 'So, ahhh, are you going to be all right?' he asked.

A weird mixture of anger, embarrassment, determination and relief combined inside me and I knew that the answer to Alvis's question was a resounding 'yes'.

'You won't have any problems with me, I promise you.' He looked relieved and no more was said. The group now down to three, we gathered our bags and moved on. We carried on in companionable silence the rest of the afternoon. When the cool of the evening came, my steps felt suddenly freer. My backpack seemed a little lighter. I began to notice the beauty of the surrounding landscape and I realised that all my other emotions had subsided and the only one left was relief.

As I lay under the thousands of stars of the desert sky that night, I wondered where Paul was and I wondered if he, too, was looking at the stars. I sent him a goodnight kiss and hoped he'd be OK before I drifted off into a surprisingly peaceful sleep.

A few hours later, at three o'clock the alarm went off. It was damned cold and I had to force myself to get up and get going. Those first few minutes after I woke were hard as the realisation of what had happened the previous day came to me. But as hard as that was,

I knew I had to block my emotions until I got out of the desert. If we made it out safely, I'd have plenty of time to mourn the end of my relationship with Paul and to work my way through conflicted feelings but right now I couldn't think about it.

Uncharacteristically, Gunther complained and said he wanted to sleep for another couple of hours. Alvis, who was clearly drained by the events of the previous day, agreed. I was disappointed because I knew that the early morning was the best time to be moving but I realised that the wheels had already nearly fallen off the whole expedition because of me so I was in no position to argue with them. I just climbed back into my sleeping bag and wakefully waited until they were ready to go. It was another four hours before we got moving.

Because we'd had such a late start, Alvis pushed the pace for the rest of the day. By nine the sun was already unbearable and an hour later we had to stop and take a break. Gunther was starting to fall behind and by the time he reached us it was clear the pace was too much for him. Alvis promised to go a bit slower but even then it wasn't long before the pace was too fast for Gunther again. Gradually, he fell further and further behind and Alvis didn't let up.

I hung stubbornly in behind him, refusing to let him get away ahead from me. There was no way I was going to hold us back. What I couldn't work out, though, was where he'd got all his energy from for the day. I didn't know that during the night, the dehydration had got so much for him that he had drunk his entire day's ration of water in one go. He was fully recharged and we were flailing in his wake.

Until now, I'd managed to stick to my one and a half litres of water a day. Some days I'd given the extra half litre to Paul but now I didn't have to worry about doing that anymore and I was beginning to suffer physically from lack of water.

Whatever troubles I had, Gunther's were worse. Every time I looked behind me he seemed to be getting further and further away. I started to worry about him. A little while later, Alvis and I found a spot of shade in a shelf on a rock face and we decided to take a break. We'd already covered 30 kilometres that day and were quietly content with our achievement. We'd been resting for about 15 minutes when we realised that Gunther was nowhere to be seen. Alvis left his pack with me and went back to look for him.

I lay there in the shade too tired to move. My feet were causing absolute agony and the skin on my shoulders where the straps from my pack pressed in was numb and bruised. Little did I know then that the feeling in parts of my back wouldn't return for another six months. My back was in a bad way. My old injuries had been exacerbated — a disc had been pushed out of alignment by the constant weight of my pack. Everything was so out of whack that I couldn't stretch my arms backwards.

As I lay in that little piece of shade, I drifted off to sleep briefly and dreamed of a huge bottle of Coca-Cola that was standing at the other end of the desert waiting for me. I woke up feeling even thirstier than I had before and decided to drink half a litre of my precious water. I drifted off to sleep again but woke a few minutes later in a blind panic. Alvis and Gunther were still not back. What if they didn't come back? What if I was alone out here? Could I get myself out? Could I help them if they were in trouble? The consequences of us being separated seemed dire, indeed. Thankfully, before I'd convinced myself that I'd been abandoned I spotted them walking towards me about half a kilometre away.

Alvis was carrying Gunther's pack and Gunther was walking

very slowly behind him. He was extremely dehydrated. Alvis had found him sitting in the sand, disoriented and exhausted. He had lost sight of us and pretty much given up. A long rest was needed. Gunther had to drink and recover so we decided to stay put until four that afternoon before walking another long stage in the cool of the evening.

By now I had recovered a little and took a good look at where we were. It was magic, a gold and white valley with bizarre formations. There were strange, black, perfectly round stones on the ground intermingled with pieces of crystal. I had the strong feeling we were the only humans to have set foot in this place for hundreds, maybe even thousands, of years. I felt privileged and humbled at the same time to be in such a majestic place. The air was completely still and burning hot, nothing moved, nothing lived — no snakes, no scorpions, no insects, no plants, no birds. Nothing could survive in this harsh climate.

Before long though, my thoughts returned to slightly less lofty things. I decided that it was time to get an idea of just how bad my feet really were. I took off my boots and my socks and subjected them to the light of day for the first time in a while. It wasn't pretty. My toenails were all either black or slowly turning black. My heels were giant blisters and there were various other blistered spots all over the rest of the skin.

I took out my first aid kit and decided to operate. A single blister covered the entire Achilles tendon area on my right heel. I knew that the only thing for it was to drain the blister. For a moment I hesitated before sticking the needle into the blister. It wasn't pain I was worried about, it was losing all that water from my body. If I could have found a way to store that water after I'd drained the blister, I would have.

In went the needle and the blister was so tight that I managed to squirt myself in the eye when the needle finally broke through all those layers of skin. The blister was so big that it took nearly half an hour to completely drain it. What remained was a floppy bag of overstretched damp skin so I left my foot out in the sun for a while before I plastered it as well as I could with what I had. I knew that whatever I did, that sock wasn't coming off until we made it to the end of the trek so it'd better be good.

While I was operating on my feet, Gunther was gradually regaining his strength and by late afternoon we were ready to get moving again. Alvis and Gunther had just enough water to last another two days so we had to cover as much territory as we could. I still had 11 litres of water in my pack but they didn't know that. I just felt that I needed to keep some in reserve in case something did go wrong.

We walked on into the night and even though I couldn't see, I could sense the landscape changing around us as huge sandhills loomed ahead of us. We managed to weave in and out of the hills only being able to see a couple of metres in front of our noses. Survival was a matter of putting one foot in front of the other. I was mesmerised by the white flicking of Alvis's heels in front of me, providing me with an orientation point. Suddenly, Alvis's heels were no longer there for me to follow. He had stepped over a small dip and disappeared and I suddenly realised how easy it would be to lose sight of him altogether. I hurried to catch up and disappeared over the same drop as suddenly as he had.

For the first time, I realised that Gunther wasn't right behind me. I looked quickly back and there was nothing but darkness. I called out to Alvis asking him to slow down and telling him that we'd lost

Gunther again. The pace had been too fast and Gunther had fallen behind. Thankfully he wasn't too far away, just far enough that we couldn't see him.

We stopped and waited and I breathed a sigh of relief as I saw his silhouette appear over the ridge behind us. That fright was all it took to make Alvis declare it a day and we set up camp in the sand. But our hopes for a restful night's sleep were soon dashed.

The evening had been unusually warm and there hadn't been a breath of wind. As we settled into our sleeping bags a sharp gust of wind took us by surprise. That gust was followed by more and each one got stronger. Minute by minute, the wind increased until it was impossible for us to ignore it. We packed up all our gear and moved to a sheltered spot behind a nearby sandhill.

As soon as we were settled in again the wind turned into a storm, a sandstorm. I huddled down into my sleeping bag and pulled the hood right up over my head, shutting the opening as well as possible. The wind lifted the sand up in bucketfuls and sprayed it on us. Inside my haven it sounded like rain on the roof and I caught myself wondering what it would be like to be buried alive. Now and again I stuck my nose out to get air. The sand was everywhere and in everything, my nose, my ears, my hair, my mouth and all through my sleeping bag and backpack. Nothing was safe. The storm continued into the small hours of the morning and when it finally subsided around 3.30 am. I heard Alvis rustling around outside.

It was time to get up. Another night had passed without sleep. I pulled my aching and tired body out of the sack and got going, feeling very wobbly on my feet. Last night I had hardly drunk anything due to the sudden sandstorm and now my thirst had seemed to disappear and it was so cold I could only drink a little before starting off. It was a warning sign I should have recognised — *lack of thirst when you're already dehydrated is a sign that your nervous system is no longer functioning properly.*

Alvis again set a swift pace in the darkness of the early morning. He was determined to put at least 30 kilometres behind us before the sun again beat us into submission. Our goal was to reach the Bawiti Depression by midday. It was a landmark that we could recognise easily on our map and I knew that if we could make it there the worst of the journey would be behind us.

An hour passed and I started to feel very strange, my vision went blurry and my legs felt weak. Suddenly everything went black and I collapsed. I woke up moments later to find myself lying like a turtle on its back unable to get up. The others put me back on my feet. 'You ok?'

'Yeah,' I said, not really knowing what had happened. We continued on in silence. Five minutes later everything went black again and I collapsed. Again, they put me on my feet and we kept going. I was annoyed. 'What's the matter with me? Pull yourself together', I told myself and I tried to concentrate. Again my vision blurred. I kept going but half an hour later I collapsed for a third time. This time I was really disoriented. I obviously needed water quite badly but Alvis didn't offer to stop and I was either too proud or too confused to ask.

I got back on my feet, gritted my teeth together and carried on. I collapsed a fourth time. By now it was routine for me and automatically I struggled up and carried on. Then finally we were there, before us lay the Bawiti Depression. We had reached the end of the mountain plateau.

What we saw before us was a completely different landscape.

The desert was no longer white, but black. We walked to the edge of the cliff and searched for a way down. By now I was extremely disorientated and hallucinating. The rocks were dancing in circles around me then turning into monsters. No matter how hard I tried I could not focus. Alvis discovered a way down, took me by the hand and coaxed me down step by step, ordering me to go on when I hesitated. The way was steep and I felt completely uncoordinated. I focused on his voice and followed his steps.

Finally, we were down. I threw my pack on the ground, ripped it open and tore out the closest water bottle I could find. I reckon that was the most important bottle of water I have ever had. A half a litre disappeared like nothing and I lay down on the ground to recover. My vision was spinning as if I was drunk.

'Everything OK, Lisa?' asked Gunther.

'Yeah, I'll be back to normal in a tick,' I answered. I could feel the water filling every dried out cell in my body. I drank a little more and rested. Alvis sat down beside me and encouraged me to drink as much of the extra water I was carrying as I could.

'There's an old Bedouin saying,' he told me. 'It's better in your tummy than in your pack.' Immediately I understood what he meant. It was easy to get obsessed with water rationing. People have died of thirst in the desert with 20 litres of water still in their bags. From now on I would drink my two litres a day because there was always a risk that my nervous system would become too damaged to recover if I kept denying myself water.

We took stock of our position. Things were looking up. It had been a hard couple of days but they had paid off. By the next night, with a bit of luck, we could be out. A feeling of anticipation and elation overcame me and for a moment I almost forgot we still had a long way to go. I hadn't expected that the sense of nearly having completed the trek would make that afternoon even harder than the ones we'd already survived. Somehow, with the tension and pressure gone, every step seemed to take twice as long.

Late that afternoon Alvis called out a single word — trees. A tiny oasis came into view. There were trees and there were people and that could only mean one thing — water. As if mesmerised, my eyes stayed fixed on that tiny point of hope far off on the horizon. The minutes passed like hours, the trees never came closer and I began to wonder if we had all been hallucinating the same thing. Eventually we arrived and I could touch beautiful green leaves. The colour put me in a trance — life. I picked a leaf. It was from a member of the eucalyptus family and it smelt heavenly.

Alvis tried to take a GPS bearing but the unit wouldn't work. It was probably because we were still in a military controlled zone and the satellites were being jammed by the soldiers. We walked into the oasis in search of water and found two men working in a garden where water ran through in canals to irrigate the plants. Alvis greeted them. Completely taken by surprise, they greeted us warmly.

We must have looked a sight because they immediately offered us water. We gratefully accepted and followed them to a spring where we were offered a cup to drink from. In turn we each drank our fill from the lukewarm water that gurgled out of the earth. None of us managed more than a litre. Our stomachs simply couldn't hold any more.

We thanked our hosts and took our leave wanting to disappear as quickly as possible. We had to get out of sight again before there could be any trouble — for them or for us. Their hospitality was very touching and I'm still surprised that they weren't suspicious of us or curious as to why we had turned up out of the desert.

The oasis was blocked on the other side with dried out salt lakes and swamps. After making our way through the driest of landscapes for the last few days we found ourselves trudging through soggy wet mud with a thick salt crust on top. Alvis charged right in, in a hurry to get out, but the ground got soggier with each step until our great leader got stuck in the mud.

I was not far behind him, but being lighter I didn't sink in so far. He struggled to free himself but by the time he managed to free one foot the other was completely trapped. I couldn't help it and I started to laugh. This annoyed Alvis no end and made him fight harder to get out, which caused him to fall over. Gunther and I completely lost all control and laughed ourselves stupid at the sight of Alvis flailing in this swamp. That just made him even more angry. 'We have to disappear, this is no laughing matter.'

He was right, of course. We were dangerously close to civilisation and where there were people there were bound to be soldiers. Biting my lip, I offered Alvis a hand and step for step we made it back on to dry land. What a sight, the 'great master' covered in mud in the middle of the desert. Gunther and I looked at each other; we didn't dare make a noise. We hopped back into line and marched on in silence for a long while.

The landscape here was a stark contrast to what we had been walking in. The sand was covered by black rocks and black volcano-shaped mountains were everywhere. I was astounded and fascinated with the beauty of the place, but the stones were incredibly uncomfortable on my tender feet.

We walked until late in the evening, motivated by the thought this could be our last night in the desert. Like a greyhound with a rabbit before its eyes, I hurtled forward with the vision of a chilled bottle of Coca-Cola in my mind. We finished that day with just 45 kilometres left to cover before making it to Bahariya and safety. We knew we would be out the next day and that helped me to sleep better.

The final day of our desert adventure started at 6 am. None of us had any problems getting motivated to get up and get going early that morning. The end of the trek was getting closer with every step we took. As we walked, we talked about what we would do once we got out and got home. Even though my return home was shrouded with uncertainty, the atmosphere was relaxed and although we still had a long way to go we didn't care.

My backpack felt as light as a feather. My legs felt strong and fit. The kilometres ticked by without me even noticing. Even my feet didn't seem to hurt that much. I wondered at what a powerful influence the psyche has over the body. It was amazing to me that when I had a positive attitude and was able to focus and find an inner rhythm, anything was possible. But the opposite was also true. When I felt negative, undecided or distracted, even getting out of bed could become too much of an effort. This discovery has held me in good stead time and time again since I first noticed it out there in the Libyan Desert.

The only thing that mattered now was getting to Bahariya and the end and this goal energised me beyond belief. As we got closer to the oasis town, my thoughts began to stray towards Paul for the first time since the night he left me in the desert. What would happen with us? As soon as this thought popped into my mind I lost my rhythm and felt like I didn't want to reach the end. I didn't want to return to the complications of everyday life. I didn't want to have to deal with whatever fallout was awaiting me when I got back to civilisation.

More than that, I didn't want to see cars and streets. I didn't want to hear music and people. I wanted to remain here in the untouched wilderness, in this beautiful, serene and deadly place.

Towards evening we finally saw the lights of the oasis on the horizon. I felt sad. The Coca-Cola bottle that I had fantasised about for so long had lost its magic. This discontentedness confused me. When I was on tour, be it in the mountains, the desert or the forest, I always longed for the comforts of home. Then once I got home I knew I'd long for the freedom to move, to be going somewhere, for the nature, the beauty and the satisfaction of being on tour.

The lights of Bahariya oasis came closer and closer. It was night time as we approached. Already rubbish and other signs of humanity were starting to appear. As we neared the oasis the three of us fell silent. We couldn't risk being seen and caught by the military who have a control point in every oasis.

Standing just outside the oasis, excited and elated, we congratulated each other. We had done it. But our celebrations were premature. None of us had noticed we were standing only 50 metres away from a military look-out tower. We quickly ducked down behind a wall. 'What do we do now?' whispered Gunther.

'We'll have to find a way through the wall somewhere and into the village,' came Alvis's reply.

While the two of them discussed possibilities, I popped the last lolly I had into my mouth and sucked on it. I had saved it until the end and here we were.

We crept along the boundary wall looking for a way in. Without finding anything we realised that we would have to pass right under the tower. We managed to sneak by right under the noses of some Egyptian soldiers and found a hole in the wall.

The three of us climbed through the hole and into a paddock where a surprised looking donkey was standing. After that, we scaled another couple of walls and found ourselves inside the village amongst the houses. We were safe.

The locals were shocked to see us but once again, the wonderful sense of Egyptian hospitality came to the rescue. A few of the local men guided us to the centre of this dusty little town and a building with a sign outside. On that sign was one of the most magical words of all: HOTEL.

The three of us walked straight in and checked in. Our room was very simple and slightly grubby but it was absolute luxury. We had really made it. We had traversed the Libyan Desert and lived to tell the tale. I lay on the bed feeling exhilarated and relieved.

The danger of the last hour now struck me and I shuddered. But it wasn't long before that fear subsided and I managed to focus my thoughts on another all important goal — that long-awaited bottle of Coca-Cola. Together, Alvis, Gunther and I marched through the town as if we owned it. We were proud and happy. Despite all the difficulties we had encountered we knew we made a good team. We found a little shack with a sign outside saying 'Café'.

'Six Coca-Colas please,' Alvis ordered for us, 'and something to eat.' As the man handed us our two bottles of Coke each we looked at each other with pride.

'Cheers comrades. We did it!' said Alvis with a smile that reached from one ear to the other.

That first drink almost brought tears to my eyes and I savoured every drop as it passed down my parched throat. Already the dinner was being served. A type of ragout with a big piece of meat in it, rice, flat bread and veges. It was a simple meal but it was heavenly. After a couple of mouthfuls I was full — my stomach had shrunk from eating very little over the previous week.

We sat back enjoying a few more bottles of Coke and discussed our plans for the next few days. Our flight from Cairo back to Vienna didn't leave for another week. At about this time, I started to worry about Paul again. Had he made it out? Was he safe? I hoped to have an answer soon.

Later that night, we returned to our hotel and as I lay on the bed I felt a sense of relief. I could finally relax and let my body begin to heal itself. But with that relief came a tiredness and an emptiness I couldn't understand. The goal that had obsessed me, pressured me and driven me was no longer there. I had a strong, almost unbeatable, desire to turn around and walk back out into the desert.

Being in the desert I had been able to turn my back on the pressures and concerns of daily life. I hadn't had to worry about money, work, society or expectations. Even though the experience had been brutal at times, my life had been reduced to the absolute necessities. All I had to focus on was survival and everything else had become peripheral.

I was scared to return to a world where my senses could be dulled again by a comfortable lifestyle. I dreaded being bombarded again with a thousand messages every day that were utterly meaningless to me. But there was no choice, I was not born a Bedouin nomad in the Sahara but as a Maori woman in New Zealand and I only knew our world, society and culture. I could only live in these circumstances a short time. It was not my home, or what I knew. With these thoughts I drifted into a deep sleep.

Early the next morning, I left the others sleeping and went to change some money at the hotel reception. As I reached into my purse

The three musketeers – me, with my brothers Mitchell and Dawson.

Climbing the Grossglockener mountain pass in Austria. It was gorgeous but freezing!

Struggling through a storm in Styria, Austria. Note the trusty good ole PVC raincoat.

Riding on flooded roads in Djerba, Tunisia.

Checking out the view of a salt lake near the Tunisian border with Algeria.

A brief rest stop near Ksar Hallouf in southern Tunisia.

Crossing the Libyan Desert in borrowed boots.

Me following Alvis and Werner on our trek through the Arabian Desert.

Blending in with the locals in Jordan where I ran the 168 kilometre Desert Cup.

At the finish line of the Desert Cup in Petra, Jordan.

At one of the rest stops for the Marathon des Sables in Morocco.

The landscape in Morocco provides plenty of challenges for desert runners.

On a mission – me and Gerhard Lusskandl three days into the Marathon des Sables.

At the end of the marathon, Gerhard had to have an operation to remove sand from his cornea.

to get the money out, I felt someone tap me on the shoulder. I turned around to see Paul standing there.

'Oh, um, hi. You're out,' I said. His presence there had surprised me and for a moment nothing more passed my lips. It was clear that we both felt awkward. I wanted to hug him. I was relieved he was OK, but this wasn't the right place for the conversation we needed to have. So, I followed him back to his room — he was in the same hotel. We exchanged small talk about what we had done and when we had got out. When I started to talk about our plans for the next few days, his face turned cold and his manner tense. I felt the pressure building and I couldn't wait any more.

'And what is with us?' I asked. After hours of discussing, arguing, crying and tension I finally got an answer to my question. We agreed we would part after an intense, exciting, turbulent and adventurous relationship that had been the centre of my life. We were both sad and hurt.

Paul pretended to be hard and cold and I just gave up, I couldn't fight any more. For months our relationship had been rocky and time and time again we had been on the brink of breaking up but something had always kept us together. This time it was too much for me.

I needed to stay true to the decisions that I'd made out there in the desert the night Paul left me. The desert had given me the right to take my life back under control and had empowered me to let go despite the hurt. We would just have to get through the next few days here together until our flight left. Once we got back to Vienna I would pack my things together and leave for home as soon as possible.

Later that day Alvis and Gunther joined us for a meal. The tension in the air was modified only by attempts to be polite to one another.

We were going to be stuck together for the next seven days, so we had to make the best of it. After all we were in an exotic location on holiday and there were many things to see and do. We decided to spend four days in the oasis exploring before returning to Cairo to visit the usual tourist attractions.

Alvis had been in this oasis twenty years before and he had met a local man named Abdul Wahab. On the day he had met Abdul it had rained for the first time in over 20 years. Abdul had found that remarkable and he had told Alvis that he must be very special and that he would not forget him. Alvis wanted to find Abdul again. We asked after him everywhere and were eventually led through the backstreets of the oasis to his house. Abdul was delighted to see Alvis and immediately offered us a tour of the village. A quiet gentle man with a wife and six children aged between eight and twenty. He was a watchmaker and he made a good living from his work.

On our tour he took us through the backstreets and we explored in detail the bubbling hot water springs that provided water for the people and the date palm plantation of more than 100,000 trees that provided the people with food and a green habitat to live in.

At the edge of the oasis were a number of salt lakes surrounded by swamps. Life blossomed here, with insects, birds and animals in stark contrast to the lifelessness only a few kilometres away. I marvelled at the power of water and at the delicate balance of such an ecosystem. If the water ran out life in the oasis would be over.

Abdul led us through a maze of gardens hidden under the date palms and explained how each family owned a small area where they grew their food. Throughout the plantation ran a maze of irrigation canals providing water for the trees and plants. The air in this jungle was moist and hot and as we wandered through I felt weak and unwell. The dryness of the desert air had made the heat bearable but here the air felt heavy to me.

Our tour led further on to brick-making sites where bricks were fired for the building of houses. I had taken over the job as photographer from Paul. Everything was photographed to document life in the oasis. With the advantage of having a local to guide us I was able to photograph the cheeky children who followed us, the old men in their traditional dress and the otherwise camera-shy Islamic women of Abdul's family to my heart's content. It was a photographer's dream.

In the afternoon Abdul took us back to his house where I was left in the kitchen with his wife and children while the men drank tea in the main room of the simple dirt-floored house. The children were excited by my presence and by the camera. I was dragged everywhere to photograph everything from the neighbours' houses and the school, to every child in the neighbourhood. Abdul's wife, a short happy lady with lovely smiling eyes invited me to drink tea with her. With no verbal communication Abdul's wife and children tried to make me feel welcome. We sat on the floor in the kitchen and attempted to communicate with each other.

After a while she took me by the hand and led me outside taking with her on the way two live chickens sitting in a basket by the kitchen door. With great pride she took the two chickens and slaughtered them in front of me, slitting their throats before throwing them on the ground to bleed to death. I was shocked at their sudden and brutal death and wondered what was happening. With the help of sign language I managed to understand we were invited to dinner and that she would like me to help pluck and cook the chickens, something that she understood to be a privilege and a gesture of friendship.

Being a supermarket-dependent Westerner I had never plucked a dead chicken and had no desire whatsoever to do so now but I didn't want to offend her. What to do? I smiled and followed her back into the kitchen with the half dead chickens still kicking on a plate. Suddenly Paul was standing in the doorway. 'How is it going in here?' he asked.

'Ah thank goodness you are here, you have to rescue me, she wants me to pluck these chickens,' I said.

'Ha, just your cup of tea! OK, I want to go back to the hotel anyway. I'll go and tell Alvis,' he said. Five minutes later all three appeared to rescue me. We returned to the hotel to rest and clean up before dinner.

At dinner, my stomach was churning at the thought of having to devour the two helpless, sweet chickens. I didn't want to appear ungrateful. For the Wahab family this was a great sacrifice, they had killed their only chickens in order to prepare a feast for us, the honoured guests. Their generosity certainly touched me.

That evening I was given honoured status in that I was allowed to eat with the men. Abdul and the four of us were seated at the table while his wife and children served us before returning to the kitchen where they were to eat. A feast had been prepared and I wondered how on earth they had managed to get all the ingredients. The meal was superb and very generous with homemade bread that was stored, dried and then soaked in water before being served. We dipped our bread into the different sauces and dishes. When we had all been overfed Abdul invited us to go bathing in the hot pools, a ritual usually reserved only for men, but he assured me that in the darkness and with the appropriate clothing, I could join them.

I wasn't sure at all but Alvis gave me the OK and I was dying to sit in the hot water so I joined them. Perhaps, I thought, the other men won't notice I am a woman in the darkness. The water was hot, unbelievably hot, so hot that none of us managed to get right in. Inch by inch we let ourselves slowly submerge up to the hips, while the Arab men jumped right in and played in the water.

As I sat on the edge of the pool I felt the stares of the other men and started to feel uncomfortable. Perhaps it hadn't been a good idea after all so I decided to hop out of the water. In the darkness I tried discreetly to get dressed. Suddenly, I was surrounded by three young men who made conversation with me in English. Politely I answered their questions. 'Are you married?' they asked.

'Yes,' I answered.

'Where is your husband?'

'Over there,' I pointed to Paul. Here it was a good idea to say you were married whether you were or not.

'Does he do karate?' With this question I started to feel very uneasy. One of the men touched my hair, another grabbed my breast. I politely pulled away and called to Paul and Alvis who came over and rescued me discreetly accompanying me back to the pools.

Abdul led us back home unaware of the incident and I walked in between Paul and Alvis kicking myself for being so naïve and thanking my lucky stars I had been born in the Western world. The lack of freedom for women in this part of the world would, for me, be unbearable. Our gracious host Abdul and his family bid us goodnight and we thanked them for their hospitality before taking our leave for the night.

The next day Paul and I explored every nook and cranny of the oasis. We tried to be civil to each other but it was clear that neither of us wanted to be there any longer than we had to. We had things to settle at home and the waiting brought only frustration and stress. I wished this whole unpleasant break-up was already over. My future was uncertain. Paul and I had made all our plans together. Our attitude to life and the way we wanted to live was the same.

Now everything was turned on its head and I felt tired. My backpack had been light in comparison to the load I was now carrying. The energy and fight that had brought me through the desert had left me and the desert itself had taken its toll on my resources. The minor problems like blisters and fallen out toe nails would soon heal without permanent scars but the dehydration had done more damage than I realised.

With still four days to go until our flight back to Vienna we returned to Cairo. Another sandstorm accompanied our departure and the air in the bus was filled with a fine dust that made breathing uncomfortable. I peered out the window as we left the oasis, a thousand memories rushing through my mind. It felt good to be back on the road again.

That afternoon we arrived in Cairo amidst the continuing sandstorm. The city seemed even more chaotic than ever with its wind-chased residents darting everywhere. After a very long taxi ride we found our way back to our hotel, collected the things we had left at reception and went out to explore the streets. As the expedition was over and we hadn't eaten much all day we decided to risk a bout of belly problems and ate in a street café where the locals ate. Falafels and bread followed by fresh pressed orange juice all at the cost of a few cents.

The next day we hoped to visit the famous pyramids but instead we spent the time changing our flight tickets in order to get home earlier then fighting our way through a huge bazaar searching for an orange juice press. We then went and visited the centre of Islamic life in Cairo, the Muslim University. Being a woman I couldn't go inside so instead I sat at the door with my shoes off and a scarf over my head next to an old man with no teeth and a smiley face. While I was waiting there I started to feel decidedly unwell and was glad for a moments' rest.

The next day as I sat in the plane on the runway at Cairo airport and waited four hours until take-off, I felt the first cramps of a bout of dysentery, which was about to make the trip home hellish. It seemed an almost fitting end to such a turbulent adventure.

How to deal with blisters
Blisters can be horrendous and they can sometimes cause blood poisoning, but they can generally be worked through though. Yes, you're walking on an open wound but once you start moving and you've been going for 10 to 15 minutes the pain of a blister will lessen. Once you stop and rest and then start again — that's when the blisters are excruciating. Like most pain symptoms they're always worse when you've stopped and are getting started again. Once the body starts to warm up again and loosens up, you should be fine.

I've had some horrendous blisters in my time and there are varying theories on how you should deal with them when you're running. Here's what I do:

➜ *Pop the blister, drain it as much as I can and gently smooth the skin back down flat.*

➜ *Next, put some drying powder on it and tape it back up. When I'm in the desert, to avoid more sand getting in my blisters, I tend to treat them then tape them up and leave them. I try not to touch them then until I've finished the race to avoid reopening them.*

➜   *I wear Injinji socks. They've got toes in them and they're fantastic to stop the rubbing between your toes and they draw the moisture away from your feet.*

➜   *The real key with blisters is keeping them clean. If you don't then you're risking blood poisoning.*

Trekking in the desert

In a desert environment, with temperatures over 40°C, it is completely inadvisable to drink only two litres of water a day. Chocolate and nuts aren't ideal food for a desert trek. Borrowing boots from someone else isn't smart. Kids — don't try this at home!

Packing for an expedition

Work out how much water you need every day and make sure you take it. A GPS system is great but they use heaps of battery power. You'll be carrying those batteries and it'll add plenty to the weight in your backpack. Always take a compass as a back-up.

CLOSE ENCOUNTERS OF THE BEAR KIND

With faith in yourself you can overcome any obstacle

Once I got back to Vienna the true damage my body had sustained in the desert soon became apparent. After I finally recovered from the stomach upset from eating street food in Cairo I found that my digestive system still wasn't functioning properly. My kidneys had been severely damaged through the dehydration. One kidney was twice the size of the other and the function of both of them was impaired. The doctor gave me a course of antibiotics to try to reduce the inflammation that, thankfully, worked but even now I still have a slight impairment in the function of one of my kidneys.

The damage to my spine was worse than I first thought. It was another six months before the muscles in my back began to function anything like normally and it was several weeks before my feet looked like they were supposed to.

Quite apart from that, I had nowhere to live and knew no one in the city except Paul. Thankfully, the people I had met on the Arabian Desert trip scooped me up and helped me get back on my feet. One of the women, Barbara, invited me to stay with her and I happily accepted. I'd also made friends with another guy on the trip, Werner, and he provided a shoulder to cry on.

I had no one else in the entire city and Paul had organised my whole life for me for years. Suddenly Werner was there looking after me and complimenting me. Unsurprisingly, given what I had just been through with Paul, all I wanted was for someone to look after me and Werner was there to do exactly that. When Paul found out that I was seeing Werner he was furious, even though he had told me that he didn't want to be with me and that he never wanted to see me again. As soon as we got back to Vienna and I started to make a life for myself he changed his mind. He was extremely jealous. He couldn't believe that I actually did leave him.

I was completely numb. I didn't know what I wanted. I couldn't feel anything. I don't think I was in love with Werner but I wanted someone to be nice to me. He treated me so nicely that all the emotions I had kept down inside me came pouring out. Paul hadn't let me wear a dress or try to be beautiful. I felt guilty wanting to be feminine again, but I loved it.

Part of me still loved Paul, too. He made me feel so guilty and he put himself firmly in the role of the victim. He was constantly telling me he didn't realise how much he loved me. There was still a kernel of the dream of us being together and happy that I held onto.

A few months after I'd made all those promises to myself in the Libyan Desert, here I was planning another trip with Paul. We decided to do a make-or-break trip through Canada and Alaska. Pretty much as soon as I agreed to go with him, he'd booked plane tickets for us both to Vancouver. From there we trained and hitched our way to Kluane National Park in the south-western corner of Canada's Yukon territory. The park is right on the border with Alaska and is dominated by the St Elias mountains. It's about the same size as Switzerland and is home to numerous massive glaciers. It's absolutely beautiful.

Like a lot of wilderness spaces in Canada, the park was home to numerous bears. We had to be really careful to follow all the park rules to do with bears. We never slept in clothes we ate in, we kept all our cooking stuff away from our tent and we made sure that all our food was stored in air-tight bear-proof containers.

Kluane was amazing in that it was so huge and there was hardly anyone there. We had the place almost to ourselves apart from a party of trampers who were walking behind us. For some stupid reason they'd brought their dog with them. As in New Zealand, in Canada it's illegal to take a dog into a national park. Not only did they have a dog, but they didn't keep it under control. It took off and ran up past Paul and me all the while barking its head off. It was barking at a bear that was on the side of the trail. We were in steep valley and the dog was on one side of us barking at the bear that was on the other side of us. The bear got really agitated and I could tell it was about to charge over and take on the dog.

Paul kept saying, 'Keep calm, keep calm.' I raised my hands up so the bear could tell I was a human being. We edged our way past the bear, which was focused on the dog, all the while absolutely terrified that the bear would turn on us.

While we were focused on getting away from the bear, we missed the turn off that we were supposed to take on the track. We ended up taking a wrong turn and climbed the side of this mountain. The climb gradually got steeper and steeper. Paul had gone on ahead of me and I ended up getting stuck on a cliff face. I couldn't move up and I couldn't move down. I could see two other climbers on a cliff face across the valley who looked as if they were stuck too.

I started yelling to get Paul's attention but he was at the top of the mountain watching the bear we'd encountered earlier as it stalked the trampers and their dog. He couldn't hear me because he was over the top of the precipice. I stayed on the spot crying hysterically, convinced I was going to slip down the cliff and die. I gripped on for dear life and realised that I had no choice but to try and climb further up. I managed to reach up and grab the next hand hold or I knew I would fall. Thankfully, I made the grab and was out of danger. Once I got to the top, I gave it to Paul with both barrels. He'd been oblivious to the whole thing, distracted by the incredible glaciers and the bear.

From the top we could see that the bear was still following the group with the dog. It was really aggressive and was acting pretty weirdly. When we got back to the base, we found out that the bear had followed them all the way back to camp. Incredibly, it didn't attack them. The park rangers had the guys arrested for taking the dog into the park. They then had to shut the park so that they could go in and kill the bear because of its unusual behaviour.

When we got back down, we also ran into the two climbers I'd seen across the valley while I was stuck on the cliff. They said to Paul, 'Bloody hell. We heard your girlfriend screaming from the other side of the park. We were miles away!' They couldn't believe that Paul hadn't heard a thing.

From Kluane National Park we made our way to nearby Whitehorse. Once we got there we went to an adventure company who hooked us up with the gear we needed to embark on a new adventure. Sitting in the Prospect Yukon van to Johnson's Crossing

I felt nervous. Paul and I were about to take off on a huge canoe journey across the Yukon Territory and I'd never been in a canoe before. Paul's canoeing experience was not much more than mine so it'd be fair to say we were a couple of greenhorns heading out into one of the most daunting pieces of wilderness in the world.

Accompanying us in the van were Heiko and Fabia, two German tourists who were also planning to spend the next two weeks paddling down the Yukon. They were heading for another river and they had quite a bit of experience. Heiko seemed to notice how frightened I was and tried to teach me some paddling techniques. Not the easiest thing to do in the back seat of minivan. He was pretty patient and he tried to teach me how to make the canoe go straight, how to land it on a bank and how to avoid tipping over in white water — in other words he was teaching me the very basics. Of course, I should have tried to learn all this stuff before I left Vienna but with everything that had been going on between Paul and I that was the last of my worries.

Oh shit, I thought to myself. What have I got myself into? Until now I'd thought that my experience on a surfboard in Taranaki's famous breaks would stand me in good stead. I figured water was water, no matter where you were and if I could handle a surfboard then a canoe couldn't be all that different, could it? Of course, that kind of thinking hadn't factored in the enormity and ruggedness of the Canadian wilderness. Suddenly, the possibility of being tipped out of our canoe by a set of wild rapids and losing all our gear to the churning waters hit me. What if we have to make our way through hundreds of miles of wilderness to get back to town in just the clothes we had on when we tipped out of the boat? A bloke we'd met a day earlier in Whitehorse reckoned it had happened to him and it had taken him three weeks to get out. At the time we just thought it was another one of those tall stories that characters in bars the world over tell. But now I realised he might well have been telling us the truth.

I peered out the window of the van. It was pouring with rain and according to the weatherman on the radio the rain was set to stay for the next few days. This just made me worry even more. For once, Paul understood my concerns. 'I must have been crazy to plan an 800-kilometre long tour for our first time up.'

I tried to reassure him that everything would be all right. 'We've experienced a lot together, and have survived more than the odd difficult situation so we're bound to survive this one, too, no matter how uncomfortable it might get. In any case it'll be an adventure,' I said half-heartedly.

Canada is a land where the horizon is endless, where bears, wolves and lynx wander through the forest. It's one of the last great wildernesses of this earth and a land where one can experience heaven and hell in one day. I just secretly hoped it'd be more heaven than hell for us.

Finally, the van came to a halt and by a bridge across the Teslin River. We climbed out, got our canoe off the roof rack and piled our packs onto the ground. Heiko and Fabia shook our hands and wished us luck. They knew as well as we did that we'd need all the luck we could gather if we were going to make it to the other end of our journey. As I watched the van drive away and the sound of the motor disappeared I felt as if we'd been completely deserted. The rain had stopped momentarily and the silence was complete.

Paul and I then spent an hour packing and repacking our bags and the canoe. In a way I think we were putting off the inevitable but there's only so much tinkering you can do before you have to face up to what's ahead of you. We realised that we just had to get on with it and climbed into the canoe and pushed off into the river. At this point, the river was slower than I had imagined but the paddling was still tough. It took us a while to stop turning in circles and actually start moving forward on the river but even then we did a whole lot of zigzagging before we worked out what sort of paddling technique would keep us going in a straight line.

After just 1 kilometre I began to understand just how hard it was going to be to paddle 800 kilometres. My arms started to burn and my back was more than a little bit sore. At least we were finally underway and I started to enjoy being far away from civilisation. I started to enjoy the peace and quiet, but soon we managed to strand ourselves on a sandbank. We rocked and we rolled but nothing we did helped us free the canoe.

In the end, Paul had to get out of the canoe and into the freezing water to free us. As soon as he got in the water he was cursing and carrying on about the cold but the only other option was for us to sit there until the water rose and that could take weeks. It took us another couple of similar strandings before we worked out how best to avoid these sandbanks in the middle of the river. After that it was pretty smooth paddling.

Here and there, salmon jumped out of the water while eagles circled over our heads. Paul was in his element and made the most of the slow flowing water to spend plenty of time photographing the wildlife that we came across as we paddled. This was paradise.

After a few hours of smooth paddling we came across an island in the middle of the river. We decided it would be the perfect place to set up camp for the night. Being surrounded by water we decided, quite wrongly, that we would be protected from a surprise bear visit.

If we'd thought about it we'd have realised that bears are very capable swimmers.

Before landing though we decided we'd follow the advice in one of our guidebooks that said you should make a lot of noise so you don't surprise any bears with your unexpected presence. We must have looked hilarious as we paddled alongside the island yelling, 'Hey Mr Bear! Where are you?' and 'Bear, bear, bear, here we come.'

Having scared off any potential company, we beached the canoes. I set about preparing camp while Paul went fishing. It only took him twenty minutes to catch three small fish for our dinner. Having learned something from Paul's auntie about being a good housewife, I whipped up some bannock bread and spaghetti while Paul gutted the fish and wrapped them in tinfoil to cook in our fire. It was a divine meal and life with Paul was peaceful. This, I thought, was how I wished it could always be.

Feeling pretty happy and with a full tummy, I went and changed into my bear-safe sleeping gear. Yep, even the clothes we slept in had to be kept away from us so that the bears couldn't smell any residual cooking smells on us as we slept. Pretty much as soon as I climbed into my sleeping bag I was fast asleep.

The next thing I knew, Paul was shaking me. 'Lis, Lisa, wake up!'

I groaned and turned over to see Paul sitting up brandishing a can of pepper spray. It took me a few seconds to work out where we were and what was going on. Then I heard it. Loud footsteps outside the tent . . . Oh My God . . . I was so scared I hardly dared to take a breath.

'Do . . . do you think it's a bear?' I whispered. I desperately wanted Paul to tell me it wasn't.

'I don't know but it sounds big enough — judging from the amount of noise it's making.'

I'd heard so many stories of the damage that bears could do and I was terrified. I started to cry. 'I want to go home,' I sobbed to Paul. Really rational, I know. Paul did his best to reassure me but I could tell he was almost as scared as I was. I tried to convince myself that Paul wouldn't let anything bad happen to me but I knew full well that if the bear decided to climb into the tent with us there wasn't a damn thing he could do about it.

For a while everything went silent. I started to wonder whether we'd imagined the noise after all and I convinced myself that it couldn't have been a bear. This worked sufficiently for me to go back to sleep but only briefly. SPLASH! I woke with a start on hearing something drop into the river. 'What the hell was that? We have to get out of here. Let's escape in the canoe,' I squeaked. I didn't care that it was still the middle of the night and if there was a bear out there it was just as likely to attack us when we were loading the canoe as when we were in the tent.

Again Paul tried to reassure me. 'Shhh, it's only a fish,' he whispered unconvincingly.

'Fish? It must have been a bloody whale then.' I wasn't having a bar of it. 'It sounded more like a bear throwing a stone into the water.'

'Ahhh, yeah, bears can't throw stones,' Paul replied starting to get frustrated. 'Fleeing in the canoe is a stupid idea, too. Our clothes are hanging up a tree along with all our food and we certainly won't make it far equipped in just our underpants now will we?' Logical as ever, he continued, 'Just stay calm. The statistics say that most people who travel to Canada return home again in one healthy piece.'

'Yeah but most don't sleep on riverbanks in the middle of the salmon season where bears love to roam at night,' I countered. At this point Paul gave up trying to reason with me and we sat in silence for another half an hour, until we finally both drifted back to sleep.

The next morning we searched the riverbank for the footprints of our night time visitor. In a patch of mud near the tent we found what we were looking for. A footprint so big I could fit my whole boot in it. It turns out our fears had been justified and there had been a very large bear prowling around the island — and I still reckon he'd been throwing stones!

Paddling along the Teslin River a few days later I was struck by the way the weak late-summer sun sparkled through patches of heavy mist on the water. It was near the end of August and with every passing day, the sun took longer to win its battle against the morning cold. The leaves on the trees lining the river were starting to turn yellow and red and the first night frosts had started to set in. In a few short months, this river would be frozen solid but in the meantime the sun wasn't giving us much warmth. I was frozen and my face was hidden deep in the hood of my jacket. We'd been paddling for two hours and had just decided to take a quick break.

On a nearby riverbank, we noticed a squirrel rushing around storing nuts for the winter. Huge salmon were lying dead along the water's edge; having spawned and laid their eggs they died in the river where they had been born. This abundance of fish meant that the local bear population were gorging themselves to build up their reserves for the coming winter. This was a magical place and I felt so lucky to be here but I also knew we had another 500 tough kilometres ahead of us.

I picked up the paddle to get moving again while Paul scanned the riverbank for animals. 'Lisa, check this out.' He handed me the binoculars. I tried to focus where he'd been looking. 'See? There. Three black points moving on the horizon.'

Bears. Oh, God. Not again. I gave Paul back the binoculars and carried on paddling. A little way down the river, I saw movement on the banks again. It wasn't bears, as we had suspected, but instead there were three black wolves running across an island. 'Come on, faster!' yelled Paul, paddling to try and catch up with the wolves in order to photograph them.

Only 50 metres ahead of us, the wolves ran into the water and swam strongly through the water before running into the forest on the other side. Paul snapped away with his camera until they had all but disappeared. As the last wolf disappeared into the trees, Paul startled me by beginning to howl. I couldn't help but laugh at how seriously he tried to call the beasts back to us. He was disappointed that none of them responded to his efforts to converse with them, but one of them did stop in its tracks and look back at us. He was probably thinking, what the hell is that guy on? Paul and I just sat there absolutely motionless. We both felt so privileged to have experienced such a rare moment. All that hardship back in Vienna seemed like a lifetime ago.

Later that day we reached the old Indian village of Hootalinqua. The village is right next to the point where the Teslin River joins the mighty Yukon River. From that point, we'd be paddling the Yukon and the river is wider and faster than the Teslin. To my relief, it meant paddling wouldn't be quite so strenuous. Up until then, it had been a long slow fight for every single kilometre that we covered. Now we would cover more kilometres every day in the same amount of time with the same amount of effort, or less.

Late in the afternoon, having paddled along the Yukon, we made it to the village of Big Salmon, at the mouth of the Big Salmon River. All of this area would have been more or less unknown to anyone but indigenous people until the 1890s when the Klondike goldrushes began. With the discovery of gold, thousands of people flocked to this part of Canada seeking their fortune. During this time, Big Salmon became a supply town for the miners. Steamers would pull in here to bring supplies to the miners and all manner of private vessels plied the river bringing in men and supplies then taking out gold.

Now all that remains at Big Salmon from those days are a few slowly rotting huts and an old Indian cemetery. But out there in the middle of nowhere, we weren't as far from other people as we thought. We rounded a bend in the river and there in front of us was a huge sign saying, 'STOP — River Traveller Survey.' We did as it said and landed the canoe just as a motor boat came roaring up with a smiling man in a green uniform at the wheel. It turned out that he was a river ranger and he asked if we'd mind answering a few questions. I thought it was incredible that even all the way out here we were still in the grips of bureaucracy. That said, we were happy to tell them what they wanted to know as anything that helped them look after this beautiful wilderness was OK by us.

By the time we were finished and free to go on our way, it was already quite late so we decided to set up the tent in one of the log cabins and stay the night. We hoped that the hut might offer at least a little bit more protection from the local bears than our flimsy tent would. With the security of having even a rickety, falling-down roof over my head, I slept well that night.

When I woke in the morning, the weather was absolutely foul.

A storm had blown in during the night and by the time we got out onto the river; the wind was pretty much blowing us back the way we came. It took all of our energy to move even the slightest bit forward. And the next day it was even worse. We had hoped to reach the village of Carmacks in the next few hours but it didn't look like it was going to happen. I was gutted as Carmacks was the only contact we'd have with civilisation along the whole route. And to make matters worse, I felt absolutely terrible. I just seemed to have no energy and was just getting weaker and weaker. I was fighting the idea of giving up the tour at Carmacks, which was only halfway along our planned route.

Up until now I hadn't mentioned to Paul that I wasn't feeling well. Partly this was because he was so excited about the whole tour and I didn't want to disappoint him after coming this far. My doubts about finishing the trek evaporated as soon as the wind died down. Within three hours we saw a moose, three grizzly bears and a lynx. It was incredible. This was the real thing and Paul and I were both excited. But a couple of hours later everything changed again.

We landed the boat and were unpacking our lunch when the wind returned with a vengeance. When we grudgingly got back in the canoe, the wind was furious. The rest of the day was a fight against the forces of nature and it was all we could do to keep the canoe upright. The battle meant that I had to forget that I was feeling really unwell and just get on with the job at hand.

In the late afternoon we stopped just a few kilometres out of Carmacks. It looked like we were going to make it into town that night after all and I was stoked. While we were stopped having a bite to eat I noticed movement on a neighbouring island. At first we couldn't work out what it was, maybe a lynx or possibly a wolf. We packed up our gear, got back in the canoe and decided to go and take a closer look.

We paddled in the direction of the island and decided it was actually a wolf we could see. But it was acting really strangely. As Paul and I got closer, it didn't run away. It just stood its ground and watched us approach. Most wolves would have hived off into the forest by then.

With only 50 metres of water separating us the animal still didn't move so we took the opportunity to take heaps of photographs. Paul was delighted at having such an amazing chance to capture images of such a majestic beast. In fact, he was so excited he clicked off our last roll of film. But as we got closer and closer, the wolf still didn't move. We started to worry that maybe it had rabies or something. It should have been scared of us. Then we saw it. As we turned to paddle away we saw a canoe upturned on the riverbank about 100 metres away. Everything clicked into place. The majestic beast we had been so eagerly photographing was actually someone's pet dog!

It was hilarious. I laughed so hard I thought I'd roll the canoe, but I reckon the dog's owners would have been laughing even more if they had seen a pair of greenhorn tourists clicking off all their film taking pictures of their dog.

Paul saw the funny side of it, too, and we laughed so much that we had to land at the next island to get ourselves back under control. Eventually we stopped laughing long enough to get back in the canoe and paddle the last few hard-fought kilometres to Carmacks. We arrived there windblown and hungry, but in high spirits.

Having seen hardly any signs of human habitation for the last week or so, I was pretty excited to get to Carmacks. Anyone would think it was the big smoke or something but the truth is it's a small village with a population of about 400 people! As soon as we'd pulled the canoe up alongside the town and the adrenaline of being out on the water had subsided, I started to realise just how sick I felt. For a couple of days I'd been feeling extremely weak and if I cut off the blood supply to any part of my body, for example by leaning my arms on something, the muscles would start to cramp and my fingers would curl into a ball. I also had pins and needles in various parts of my body which made me wonder if there was some problem with my blood supply. I knew I had to face the truth and tell Paul. He was pretty understanding. 'Maybe we should wait here for a day and see if you feel better,' he suggested.

'I'm OK, but if I can't continue, will you carry on alone?' I ask.

He looked worried so I tried to reassure him that I'd be fine. 'I'll be all right alone. If you want to keep going you should. I only hope you can manage the canoe by yourself, especially over the rapids ahead.'

'I hope so, too.' I felt terrible for putting Paul's dream of paddling the Yukon at risk but I'd also learnt to take my health seriously. Having suffered long-term side effects since getting back from Egypt, I didn't want to risk being seriously ill out on the river. We pitched our tent for the night and were both pretty quiet, lost in thoughts of what we would face tomorrow.

When I woke the next morning, I wasn't feeling any better and knew that my time paddling the Yukon was over. Paul was going to have to paddle from Carmacks to Dawson City on his own. I knew that I couldn't go on. I could also tell that he was relieved that I hadn't insisted on him staying with me. Even if I couldn't finish the journey, he could.

As soon as we'd decided that I would head back to Whitehorse and Paul would continue on to Dawson City, it was all go. Paul needed to restock the canoe with food and water for the rest of the trip. I had to repack all my stuff and find a ride back to Whitehorse, which was 400 kilometres away. It didn't take long before I managed to score a seat in a van heading there and as soon as that was arranged, Paul was happy to get back onto the river. I gave him a quick hug and we set off in opposite directions.

Sitting in the van on the way back to Whitehorse, I began to regret my decision to turn back. Maybe I should have carried on. On the other hand, I knew that something wasn't right. I felt really weak and was having dizzy spells. After a couple of days' rest in Whitehorse, I wasn't feeling any better. In fact, I was sitting relaxing in a spa pool one afternoon when I blacked out. Even then, I didn't think too much of it as I had been so tired. I figured it was part of recovering from so much physical exertion. I also had a funny tingling sensation in my arms and my muscles felt quite weird, but it wasn't anything unusual for me. I just put it down to the muscle damage and circulation problems that I'd sustained while crossing the Libyan Desert.

All up, I spent a week in Whitehorse before catching a bus to Dawson City to meet Paul at our arranged meeting time. Dawson City is an amazing old goldrush town lost in the 1890s. All the buildings are Wild West-style, complete with swinging saloon doors and cancan joints. Everyone wore cowboy hats and the dusty roads were just like you see in the movies. At the same time that I stepped off the bus, Paul rounded the last bend on the river before Dawson City. Within an hour, we found each other on the main street, which wasn't very difficult given only 1300 people live there.

Paul was burnt to a cinder and grinning from ear to ear at having achieved the goals he'd set for himself. It turned out that he had come across three fellow Austrian canoeists just after leaving Carmacks. They had paddled together across some of the worst rapids on the river before Paul decided to strike out on his own as they were going a bit too slowly for his liking. The Austrians had been very glad to see him. They were three total greenhorn would-be hunters who'd gone out on the river with no food, except carrots and potatoes. They were planning to catch and kill their food — Paul taught them how to hunt and fish.

Paul seemed happy to see me. Dawson City was a real treat for both of us and we splashed out to see a cancan show and paid to stay in a weird backpackers' hut, which made a change from sleeping in our tent. I felt a bit better so we continued our journey as planned, heading up into Alaska. We hitched from Canada across to Alaska heading for Denali National Park, which is home to Mt McKinley, the highest peak in the United States. We got a lift with an old native American guy who was a wolf trapper. Paul was stoked as he'd always been fascinated by native American culture. The trapper spun us a few yarns about the old days when he hunted wolves for a living.

Sadly, the old trapper was more interested in getting into my pants than teaching Paul the ways of his people. We jumped into his four-wheel-drive and headed up a dirt track out to his village — it turned out to be pretty scary. He freaked us out by telling Paul he was a tepee creeper and it was my tepee he wanted to creep into. I reckon Paul slept with one eye open that night to protect me.

We were miles from the road and we had no way back except in the same truck we'd arrived in. These guys all had guns and we didn't know how we'd get back. Thankfully, the next morning, we managed to talk the trapper's mates into putting us into a boat and taking us back to the road. We were mighty relieved to get back to the tarmac!

Our next lift was with a fantastic family. The woman was of European descent and her husband was a native Alaskan. They took us back to their house, fed us and put us up for the night. It was wonderful to sleep in a bed for a night without having to worry about tepee creepers. We also loved having the comforts of someone's home. Before we left, the man gave me a walrus bone pendant that he'd made, which was a really special gift.

The following day we finally made it to Denali. The mountain was majestic set among the autumn trees. It was a sight I'll always remember. Denali National Park is absolutely huge. Because we only had a couple of days at the park, we did the touristy thing and took a bus ride far into the park. We hopped off the bus and disappeared further into the park to do some walks. It was magic. At 6194 metres, Mt McKinley is the highest peak in the United States and it's more than twice the height of Mt Taranaki. I was glad that Paul didn't suggest we climb it!

However, there was plenty to do in the park without tackling the mountain. There was wildlife everywhere with moose, bears and mountain goats in abundance. They didn't seem remotely interested in us so we didn't feel at all threatened being in their environment. Even though I still felt quite unwell, we weren't really exerting ourselves over this time. It was such a special time for us both. From Denali we headed out to the Alaskan coast. It was the salmon season so there were fishermen everywhere and more salmon than you could ever hope to eat. It was smoked as soon as it came out of the water and we ate it not long after. It was absolutely delicious.

While we were staying on the banks of Prince William Sound, Paul and I decided to take a day cruise out to sea as a treat. While we were out there, a huge pod of orca whales — there must have been about 50 of them — joined the ship and played around its bow for a good hour. It was absolutely delightful. As a background to the whales, there were massive glaciers creaking and carving into the ocean. What I saw that day was incredible and will stay with me for life. Staying in a coastal town on Prince William Sound, we planned to climb a nearby mountain. We'd got as far as the base of the mountain before the weather got so bad that we decided to head back to the village we'd stayed in the previous night.

As usual we were travelling on the smell of an oily rag and there were no luxuries like hotels, even if it was freezing cold and miserable. Our tent didn't offer any relief from the cold so we did what travellers the world over do when they want to warm up — we headed for the local public library. It was lovely being in the warm in a room crammed full of books. I curled up on a couch and was soon lost in a book. Before long, I noticed the tingling sensation in my arm was back. Only this time, it didn't just disappear like it had before. After a few moments, it began to intensify and spread throughout my whole upper body. I was terrified.

'Paul! Something is happening to me. Get help fast . . .' No sooner had I managed to get the words out than my body went into a seizure. My muscles all cramped but it wasn't like normal cramp. If felt a thousand times worse. Even my facial muscles contorted in a frightening fashion. I tried to call for help but my body was completely wracked by the spasms. The pain was excruciating and I remained conscious throughout the whole episode. I was absolutely convinced that I was going to die.

I had no comprehension of what was happening to me. Paul tried to stretch my arms back to break the cramps. This is a guy who could bench press 150 kilograms and he couldn't open my arms — such was the intensity of the seizure.

Luckily, there was a repair man in the library who also happened to be a paramedic. I managed to whisper that I thought I needed sugar as I had a history of hypoglycaemia. He had a sports gel that he squirted in my mouth. It helped momentarily and the muscles began to let go — but not for long, the seizure returned moments later. Within minutes an ambulance arrived and I was taken straight to the local hospital. The doctors there managed to use medication to release the seizure. I still don't know what it was but it must have been powerful stuff. They also did a whole raft of tests to try to find out what had caused such an extreme reaction.

When the test results came back, the doctor gave me some frightening news. He told me I'd had what was called a tetany seizure. He believed it had been caused by a combination of mineral deficiencies, an electrolyte imbalance, mild hypothermia and low blood sugar. It didn't seem like there was much more I could have done wrong. The main reason for the seizure was the lack of potassium in my system. According to the doctor, my potassium levels were among the lowest he'd ever seen in a person still alive. His next words rang in my ears. 'The only things that saved you from having a heart attack are your youth, your high level of fitness and the fact that you got treatment so quickly. If we hadn't been able to release you from the seizure as quickly as we did it is quite likely you would have had a fatal heart attack.'

A heart attack! I couldn't believe what I was hearing. I just felt so grateful that the seizure happened when I was in town and near the hospital. I don't even want to think about what would have happened if it had happened out on the river.

After the seizure, Paul was totally freaked out and was quite frightened for me. Thankfully, it was a problem that was easily fixed. I just had to take potassium tablets and make sure that I had good food and plenty of rest for a few weeks. It had been a very close call though.

We ended our travels in Anchorage, Alaska and from there we flew back to Vancouver for a couple of days before returning to Vienna.

Supplements, minerals and vitamins.
Something as basic as a potassium deficiency almost cost me my life. We didn't have electrolyte drinks and stuff like that back then. It's so important to take supplements when you're doing intensive exercise. The food that most people eat now doesn't supply them with all the vitamins and minerals they need.

There are plenty of supplements and vitamins available for athletes. The ones I think are vital are:
→ *Calcium, iron and magnesium, which can be depleted.*
→ *BCAAs or branched-chain amino acids, which are vital for muscle strength. The body will break down muscles while you're exercising to get stored BCAAs so if you supply your body with extra, muscles and other tissues are spared from breakdown.*
→ *Flaxseed and salmon oil are really important for lubricating joints, healing and circulation.*
→ *Electrolyte drinks are vital for any runner. Try to drink 800 millilitres of water an hour in hot climates — ideally at 200*

millilitres every quarter hour. You should always drip feed the water rather than taking huge amounts with long periods between. You should try to keep your stomach full but not over-full. Even in lower temperatures you should be aware of keeping hydration constant.

My performance-enhancing secret weapons are:

→ *In a long distance race, I should make sure that I start hydrating early on.*

→ *I always take jelly-type sweets with me for when I need a sugar hit, but I never have too many at once to avoid crashing down the other side.*

→ *Ginger ale settles my stomach, it tastes good and I get a sugar hit, but I make sure it is flat and just have sips.*

→ *Within 40 minutes of a training session, it's vital I eat something because muscles' uptake of vitamins and minerals is much faster within that time.*

A QUIET LIFE

Live in the present. The past is what it is

My on-again, off-again relationship with Paul lasted for another year. I would leave him, and then he would come after me using a combination of threatening, begging and loving words. Each time I would go back to him. My mind was a jumble of not wanting to fail in our relationship, of residual love and of plain old-school fear.

When I left Vienna to come home to Taranaki in mid-1998, it was so I could get away from everything.

When I got back to New Plymouth and to my family, I fell apart completely. I'd been trying so hard to keep everything together and when I was surrounded by the people who loved me unconditionally and who would look after me, I completely let go.

It was, without doubt, the lowest point in my life. Simple things like the phone ringing would set me off. Every time it rang, no matter what time of the day, I was scared. I was scared that it was going to be Paul calling me and I never knew if he was going to be begging me to come back or abusing me for having left.

Over that time Mum and Dad were amazing. They pretty much wrapped me in cotton wool and looked after me for six months straight. I'd spent huge amounts of time in bed, scared to get out and face the world. Gradually, I started to realise that I had plenty to live for and that hiding from the world wasn't going to solve anything. Getting back on my feet was a slow process and one that had its fair share of setbacks.

One of the things that really helped was spending heaps of time with Dad. We would go for huge long walks and we went fishing. Neither of us would say anything but just being with him helped. It must have been terrible for him as I would often be walking along bawling my eyes out. I could tell that it broke his heart that there was nothing he could do to help me. But just having him there with me was more help than he could ever have known.

Mum, too, was an absolute lifesaver. I felt like I had gone back to being a child again and she just accepted that I needed time and space to come right. She'd cook for me, clean for me and listen to me when I needed to talk. I couldn't have asked for more from either of my parents and I will always be grateful for the way that they looked after me completely and unquestioningly.

Werner followed me and arrived in New Plymouth in December 1998. It was great to see him again and he seemed to enjoy spending time in New Zealand. I decided to try to make our relationship work and, after spending some more time at home with the family, Werner and I returned to Vienna. It was pretty tough going back to Austria and knowing that Paul would be living close by. Not long after we got back, Werner bought a house about an hour outside

Vienna and we moved out of the city.

Once Werner went back to work, I realised that — for the first time in years — my time was my own and I could do whatever I liked. Apart from a short time that I spent teaching English, I had been tied up with Paul and our life and travels for years. It was time for me to do something that I wanted to do, something that I could enjoy and that I might be able to make a living from. I'd always been quite creative so I started a jewellery apprenticeship. Werner was really supportive of me doing this and it was amazing to me that someone other than family would encourage me to follow my own dreams while providing me with a safe haven to live.

My jewellery apprenticeship was the one thing that really made me happy over that time. I loved being in the workshop turning my designs into wearable pieces of jewellery. It was incredibly cathartic to have something to really focus my energy on. It was also great to have a creative outlet.

However, Werner worked long hours and we were living out in the country so my life was quite lonely. I found it quite difficult, but it did mean that I became very independent. Having spent so much time in the past few years running, cycling and tramping it was great to have the space to get back into training. Apart from jewellery-making, I spent a lot of time running. I found that going out running helped me to work through my thoughts and feelings. Gradually, I started to run further and further to clear my head. I enjoyed spending time outdoors. Sometimes I would go off for whole days at a time walking, tramping, running and biking.

When I saw an article about the Marathon des Sables in a sports magazine, it was as if a light bulb had been switched on in my head. I had been missing adventure in my life and I'd been running heaps anyway. Maybe this was something I could do? The Marathon des Sables is a 243-kilometre endurance race across the Sahara Desert in Morocco. It takes place every year in late March or early April. It takes six days to complete and as the course changes every year, no competitor ever knows exactly where it will take them.

The more I thought about it, the more I wanted to do the race. Everything I read made it really clear how difficult the race is and how you'd need to be insane to want to do it. I realised that no matter how hard it was, it would have to be easier than what I had been through in the Libyan Desert. I mean, here there'd be medics on hand, there'd be safe drinking water at every checkpoint, there'd be detailed maps and the military would be there to help me, not lock me up for life!

After thinking about it for ages and talking it through with Werner, I decided I was going to go for it. I was heading back to the Sahara and I couldn't wait. Werner was very supportive of me going to do the Marathon des Sables. There was just one thing standing in my way — money. If I was going to do it, then I was going to do it on my own and I needed to raise a lot of money to cover my costs. I quickly leapt into action finding sponsors and getting publicity. Thankfully, I was seen as a bit of a trail-blazer in Austria and people were really interested in my story and what I was planning to do.

The real breakthrough with funding came when Paysafe Card — it's a way of paying for stuff on the internet — came on board. A friend of mine in the jewellery industry, Mitra, was going out with the guy that owned Paysafe Card. She was really interested in my plans to run in the Sahara and we'd talk about it quite a bit. She went home and told her boyfriend about it and straightaway he agreed to sponsor me. I was so lucky that he got why I wanted to do the race and also that he saw the potential benefits that sponsoring me could bring to his company.

The media were really interested in what I was going to do and there was plenty of coverage about this crazy Austro–Kiwi planning to run across the desert. So, having arranged all my sponsorship money, I got stuck in and trained my arse off to be ready for the race. I couldn't wait to get back to the desert again. I was excited and scared but I was really confident that I could complete the race. I ran about 110 kilometres a week, sometimes carrying a backpack to get used to the weight I'd have to run with in Morocco.

THROUGH THE DESERT TO A NEW LIFE

When a crisis is looming, defer making any irreversible decisions

Flying down to Morocco, I began to realise the scope of the race — 700 of us running across the Sahara and about 50 of them were from Austria and Germany. There were two from Vienna and we travelled to Frankfurt to join the German team. It was great being involved in an individual sport that also had an amazing team spirit. The other guys on the team were really such great people and it wasn't long before I started to make friends, which was something I was still getting used to doing. I was rediscovering life and people again and it was great fun.

On 30 March 2001, the team flew together to Casablanca before switching to a smaller plane to Ouarzazate. After a night in a hotel there, we all got on buses and were driven for several hours out into the desert. Eventually, we got transferred onto army trucks and taken even deeper into the desert to the huge camp set up at the

Driving out to the start line of the Trans-333 in the middle of Tenere Desert, Niger.

At the start of the Trans-333 in Niger – before the food poisoning set in.

At a local school in Agadez, Niger. Several runners donated food and equipment to the school after the race.

Me behind the counter of my jewellery shop in New Plymouth.

With Chris Cruikshank, my trainer at City Fitness gym in New Plymouth just before our Death Valley campaign in 2008.

Me and Gerhard at City Fitness before our 12-hour fundraising run in April 2008.

Neil Wagstaff, Sandy Barwick, me, Chris Cruikshank and Gerhard Lusskandl at the start line of the Badwater Ultramarathon, July 2008.

At the briefing before Badwater, I managed to get my photo taken with one of my role models – Dean Karnazes.

Thanks to my generous sponsors, I had my very own billboard at the entrance to New Plymouth.

On the road during the Badwater Ultramarathon being filmed by Chris, the cameraman from *20/20*.

In pain during a moment's break from the race. I'd run about 100 kilometres at this stage and had just reached the top of the first pass.

Finally – the finish line!

Just after I finished the race with my wonderful crew Sandy Barwick, Neil Wagstaff, Chris Cruikshank and Gerhard Lusskandl.

Training in Taranaki for the next big challenge . . .

start of the race. There were helicopters all over the place, hundreds of journalists and heaps of army guys all racing around before the start of the race.

It was great to be back in the desert and know that I was safe. I would have 9 litres of water a day throughout the race and, now, I had a bunch of mates to run with. I would have a backpack that wasn't so heavy that it would cause me nerve damage. I was staggered to find out that there was a 30-strong medical team on hand as well as 250 other race personnel who had access to 90 vehicles, two helicopters, a Cessna plane and four camels. Fantastic!

It was extremely exciting just being in camp with the rest of the team. Each country was allocated a tent in camp. We all flew our own flags and there was a good-natured competitiveness between us. Everyone running the race was so interesting and there was a fantastic sense of comradeship within and between teams.

We spent two days at camp getting organised, sorting out our race numbers, packing our gear and getting medical checks, including being weighed and having our blood pressure checked. Before the race started we all got given a road book. It detailed the course the race would take and the length and terrain for each stage. None of us could wait to get our hands on them. The night before the race the organisers put on an amazing meal for all the competitors — it was simply fantastic.

The next morning we got up to start the race — it was 1 April. April Fool's Day seemed an appropriate time to start a race across the desert . . .

The race itself is made up of six stages that take place over 7 days, including one night stage. All up, it covers 243 kilometres with the stages being of varying lengths and levels of difficulty. The day that everyone feared, though, was the fourth day when we had to cover about 80 kilometres — more than double the distance covered on every other day.

All 700 of us lined up and started the race together. As soon as the gun went, everyone was off. There were helicopters flying over us filming the start adding to the excitement of getting underway at last. It sure beat the hell out of walking through the Libyan Desert on our own!

The first day was an easy 26 kilometres through to the first rest point. Even though it wasn't too tough, I spent quite a while at the first checkpoint dumping every bit of gear that wasn't absolutely essential. I even cut my toothbrush in half to minimise the weight of my pack.

Marcel, another member of the Austrian team, and I decided to run together. He wasn't quite as experienced as me, or as fit, but I was quite used to doing this kind of desert crossing with other people so I decided to stay with him.

On the third day, which was a 36-kilometre stage, Marcel collapsed and I thought his race might be over. However, he managed to get back up and get going. He was so scared that he wouldn't be able to complete the whole race I decided to stick by my word to him and we walked together. It took us absolutely ages to get to the checkpoint for the night. When we got there, Marcel was taken straight to the medic's tent where he was put on a drip to rehydrate him. Every runner was allowed one of these infusions during the race, for which they'd receive an hour's time penalty. The difference in him after he'd been rehydrated was incredible and he managed to carry on the next day.

Day four dawned very early. We knew that we'd have to cover

about 80 kilometres and it would take us most of the day and night. It was the only day of the race where we were expected to run through the night. Even as we set off that morning, Marcel was struggling. He was already exhausted but I did what I could to keep him going.

Even though I was running with Marcel the whole day, I spent a lot of time in my own head. My body was on the verge of exhaustion and I was mentally and physically right at the edge of my abilities. With all of my defences down, this was the place and time that I finally started to grieve for the life I'd planned with Paul. I spent hours walking through the Moroccan Sahara crying my eyes out over him. It was both traumatic and incredibly cathartic. This was the first time I'd been in the desert since he left me and I was finally doing something on my own, proving not only my ability but also my self-worth. I was finally able to let go of all the hurt, pain and sorrow that our relationship had caused me and, on that day out there in the Sahara, I knew that I was going to be all right.

When I finally got to the end of the stage, 19 hours after I'd set out, I collapsed in a heap. I was absolutely dehydrated — all that crying hadn't helped me store the 9 litres of water I had with me. The race marshals took me to the medic's tent and they had no choice — they put me on a drip to rehydrate me. At least I'd managed two days more than Marcel before I needed it!

Even though I desperately needed the drip, my kidneys weren't quite up to dealing with it the way they might have been before they'd been so badly damaged in Libya. The way it works is that the medics keep pumping water into you until you need to pee — that way they know that your whole body is getting the moisture it needs. The water kept going in, litre after litre, and . . . well . . . nothing was coming out again.

The tent was so busy with athletes who needed help that the medics just kept changing the bag when it got empty and in the end, I'd had 7 litres of water pumped into me before I needed to go to the toilet. I was like the Michelin man — completely bloated. It must have looked hilarious.

Suddenly, the need to have a wee hit me. I was hooked up to an intravenous drip and, because my feet were so blistered, they'd put these blue plastic bags on my feet. It must have been quite a sight. This filthy, bloated chick wearing Smurf shoes and grubby cut-off shorts wandering out of the tent attached to a drip to try and find the toilets. Then I realised — there wasn't time to find a toilet. I had to go, and I had to go right then. So I dropped my pants right outside the tent without realising that right behind where I was going about my business, there was a whole bunch of Moroccan army guys having a game of football! What was worse, by the time I realised they were there, there was no way I was going to be able to go anywhere in a hurry. Seven litres takes quite a while! I don't know who was more embarrassed, them or me . . .

As I was going with the flow, one of my teammates came over from our tent to see how I was getting on. Well, he saw all right. And he was so highly entertained by my predicament that he pulled out his camera to record the moment for posterity. I had enough energy to swear up a blue storm at him but it didn't put him off. Still, as soon as I went back into the medic's tent, I realised it could have been a lot worse. The guy in the bed next to me was hooked up to a drip as well. But he had a rather more urgent toileting problem — he needed to have a poo and he was trying to tell the doctors but he didn't speak any French. By the time they worked out what he was trying to say, it was too late. And you're only meant to have the one set of clothes for the whole race — what a terrible reason to have to drop out of the race of a lifetime. Thankfully, the medics had a scout around and managed to find the poor bugger a clean pair of pants so that he could complete the race unencumbered. The life of an ultra-athlete is *so* glamorous.

Having had the infusion, I felt great for the remaining couple of days of the race. The next day, rehydrated, I was back on form. I had a great day and I knew I was only a day away from finishing my first desert race. The final day was short — only 25 kilometres. Actually crossing the finish line was special. It was a milestone for me knowing that I'd done a race on my own.

The one regret I have about that race was that I'd stayed back and walked with Marcel for so long. In hindsight, I should have just run it on my own — staying with Marcel meant being out in the sun much longer than I needed to be. Even so, I still managed to finish in thirty-third place and I was stoked.

Once I made it over the finish line, I went to the medics to get a post-race check-up. They stuck me on the scales and I'd managed to put on 5 kilograms! I'd just spent a week running across the desert and I'd managed to put on weight. It was a bit of a different scenario from the Libyan expedition. The doctors realised there was a problem with my kidneys and gave me some diuretics to try and flush my system out. Instead of spending the day celebrating having completed the Marathon des Sables, I spent the day making a well-worn path to the toilet. I reckon I was peeing about every 20 minutes but by the end of the day, I'd dropped that extra 5 kilograms.

After our post-race checks, the race organisers piled us all into buses and drove us back to Ouarzazate. It took a few hours but it was great to be finished the race and back at the hotel. Pretty much all of the athletes were staying in the same place. I got out of my racing gear and peeled the bandages off my blistered feet, excited at the prospect of a hot shower. I hadn't been prepared for the fact that everyone else was planning on the same thing and all the hot water had been used up. My shower was freezing cold!

The hotel had a fabulous pool complex and having all spent the last week in the heat of the desert, the idea of a swim was blissful. Unfortunately, because nearly all of the athletes had come back from the race with blisters and other skin problems we were all banned from using the pool in case of cross infection. That blue water taunted us all.

After a couple of days of celebrating with my teammates, I flew back to Vienna. I made it home and in the first week back I lost another 5 kilograms as my body healed itself from the rigours of the desert. Most of this was from swelling going down and from my muscles recovering from being pushed to the edge.

Back in Vienna, I really felt like a changed person. The run through the desert had been so much more than a physical challenge. Mentally it had completely changed me and I didn't feel like I fitted into my old life anymore. It took me a month to settle and get back into the routine of everyday life. My life just seemed so decadent and full of unnecessary stuff, but I didn't know what to do about it.

Luckily, I had my team members from Morocco to talk to and I soon found out that they were going through much the same thing. Once you've experienced something that extreme and that challenging, day-to-day life seems so lacking in meaning. Being out in the desert really makes you reassess the value of your life. While you're taking yourself to the limits you start to think quite deeply about things. I knew that my relationship with Werner was in deep trouble and that it wasn't really what I wanted anymore.

I did the only thing I could think of — I started training for another desert run. This time, I was going to run the Desert Cup in Jordan. And I was going to do it in November. I had just seven months to prepare. People were amazed when I said I was going to do another desert run so soon. Seven months felt like quite a long time to me and I was excited at the prospect of running in the desert again. I was really focused on training and I did a heap of long-distance races in Austria including a 12-hour, a 24-hour and an ironman race. I needed to get as much experience as I could in endurance running to really make the most of the next race.

The thing that makes it easy for me to do races like this pretty much back to back is the massive sense of achievement I get from crossing the finish line. Crossing that finish line, the first thing I feel is relief for having completed what I've set out to do. Then I feel an incredible sense of joy for having achieved my goal. My body is depleted but slowly over the next few days a quiet satisfaction grows as I begin to focus on the good things that happened while I was out on the course. The struggles and the stresses are the price I have to pay for the victory of getting over that line and achieving the goal I've set for myself. The pain is temporary but the achievements last forever. Like any great achievement in life, it is necessary for me to put great effort in.

Dealing with heat

About 90 per cent of body heat is lost through your head, so if you're running in extreme heat it's really important to keep your head cool. This can be done with ice packs and cold water. It's important to keep your eyes, face and nose wet but this can be tricky to do without getting your shoes and socks wet!

Extreme heat can actually cook your internal organs. This can happen if you dehydrate or overheat and it can be fatal. The key is to not let your inner core temperature go over 40°C.

There are a number of reasons why runners collapse during a race ranging from hypoglycaemia, to exhaustion and overheating. If you collapse, it's vital that your crew take your temperature to establish whether you've overheated. If your temperature is over 40°C, then they need to cool you down fast. The best way to do this is to get you into icy water as soon as possible.

SAND IN MY VEINS

You must know your capabilities and expand them to the limit

When I returned to Vienna from Morocco in April the Austrian media were really interested in my story. They seemed to like the idea that this Maori girl from New Zealand had settled in their country and was running these crazy races under their flag. Mitra and her husband were happy, too. It was great in terms of raising my profile and it certainly made it much easier for me to get further sponsorship.

The biggest talk show on Austrian television, *Vera*, approached me to be a guest. I couldn't believe it. It's hosted by Vera Russwurm who is a hugely popular star — she's Austria's Oprah. It was exciting to be part of such a big TV show.

Arriving at the studios, I got whisked into the green room backstage to have my make-up done. The crew had asked me to come wearing my running gear so it was pretty funny sitting there in my shorts and sandy shoes while a stylist did my make-up. Vera came in and introduced herself about 5 minutes before the show started. Her first comment to me was 'You're not skinny enough to be a runner!' I think she'd been expecting a skinny wee marathon runner. It was a live show so there was a studio audience who were all cheering as I walked on.

I was nervous because I knew the show had a big audience, but I've always enjoyed public speaking and haven't ever been worried about getting up in front of people. On the show we talked about the expeditions I'd already completed and about my plans for the Desert Cup. Like most people, Vera was interested in why I do what I do and how I got into it. Then they showed a clip of me in the Marathon des Sables and a whole lot of photos of my other treks.

As a result of the exposure I got on Vera's show and on various other news shows, Coca-Cola Austria agreed to sponsor me to do the Desert Cup. This was unheard of. The company had only ever sponsored team sports and this was the first time they'd backed a solo athlete. The boss there was intrigued with the whole desert running thing and he really believed it fitted with the whole Coke ethos. He also knew that they'd get good media coverage out of it so he was confident they'd get their money's worth of advertising from my exploits.

Once I'd got all my sponsorship sorted, I had to focus on training for the race. I spent six months really getting into my physical preparations. For the first time, I worked with a running coach and I consulted a sports doctor. We got a heap of lab tests done and all sorts of analysis went into my physical preparation to try and maximise my running ability. I also got the Kärnten team, who run the Austrian ironman races, to write up a training plan for me. For the first time, I felt like I was going into a race with the right gear, the right supplements, support and a good health plan. It was all becoming quite professional, which took a lot of pressure off me.

As well as all this analysis and preparation, I set about taking part in every race I could find. I did a pile of 100-kilometre runs, 24-hour races, marathons and even a triathlon. It was great for my fitness but it meant that I over-trained a bit. Despite that, I reckon I was in the best shape I'd ever been in when I got to the start of the Desert Cup.

One of the great things about having confirmed sponsorship with Coke was that I was provided with a camerawoman to come with me on the run through Jordan, which would result in a documentary being made about my race.

The Desert Cup was a really tough race. It was 168 kilometres across the Arabian Desert. The race started in the desert at Wadi Rum then included a number of mountain passes before ending at the famous pink city of Petra. To complete the race means covering 104 kilometres of desert sand, 23 kilometres of ridges and valleys and 41 kilometres of mountain tracks, and involved climbing as high as 1540 metres. It was organised by the same people that did the Marathon des Sables so I knew that everything would be well taken care of. Once again, I joined the German team and we flew to Amman in Jordan, where we spent a couple of nights before heading south to Wadi Rum.

Arriving in Wadi Rum, I was once again struck by how beautiful the desert is. The landscape was stunning. The colours of the sand were different to what I'd seen before — it never ceases to amaze me how every desert looks different.

The really brutal thing about that race is that it was non-stop. I had a maximum of 62 hours to complete it, passing through thirteen checkpoints along the way. At each of the checkpoints, competitors were given 1.5 litres of water each. Other than that, we had to carry everything else that we would need along the way. At least, with the race being non-stop, I didn't have to carry a sleeping bag. After having carried 15 kilograms in my pack for the Marathon des Sables, I'd managed to cut the weight down to 12 kilograms for this race.

There were 200 of us running the race and we all started at the same time. The field spread out pretty quickly. Some of the runners were aiming to do the whole run in 24 hours, with the record being just over 21 hours. Me, I was just hoping to finish.

Even though I had a bit of desert experience under my belt, this was a whole different experience. At least on this race I had some electrolyte drinks with me but despite all the specialised training I still didn't really know what I needed to stay at optimum performance throughout the run.

The combination of my naïveté about non-stop running and having the cameras on me meant that I went out of the gates like a scalded cat. I wanted to look cool for the cameras rather than my usual slow-running self. They were with me for the first 20 kilometres so I went a whole lot faster than I should have. As the day got progressively hotter, I got more and more dehydrated. The sand was really deep so every step drained my body further.

Thankfully, the support vehicle with the camera in it couldn't follow me right throughout the race. The terrain meant that they had to take alternate routes and would meet up with me further along the trail. As soon as we got to the point where the vehicle with the camera crew couldn't follow me anymore, I crashed. I'd only covered 20 out of 168 kilometres and I'd hit the wall. My glucose stores were gone and I remember lying in the sand thinking, 'Oh f**k. I'm in trouble.' I didn't know what or how I was going to do. There was a camera waiting for me, the whole of Austria seemed to be interested in what I was doing and I'd only just managed to do one-eighth of the race.

Thankfully, as I lay there contemplating becoming a national laughing stock, a French guy came along. 'Are you all right, mate?'– or something to that effect — he asked in French. I groaned. He urged me to carry on. 'You've got to get up. You can't stop now. Come on!' I can't imagine what he was thinking — I'd only been going for a few hours! But it ain't over until the fat lady sings . . .

I wasn't very responsive so he decided to take things into his own hands. He pulled me out of the sand, put me on my feet and promised to stay with me until we reached the next checkpoint. It was only a couple of kilometres away and, with his help, I managed to get there.

Once I arrived at the checkpoint, I lay down. I spent 20 minutes sitting on my arse in the sand taking stock of where I was at. I decided the only way I could finish the race was by maintaining what energy reserves I had. When I got back on my feet, I varied my pace between a jog and a walk for the next few hours. It was time to get down to the nitty-gritty business end and stop showing off. I was still inexperienced and over-enthusiastic. Not much has changed really!

The terrain was much tougher than Morocco with the deep sand. In Morocco the sand is often hard packed so it's easy to run on. Here I found myself sinking into the sand and having to drag my feet out with every step. There were also a whole lot of sand dunes here, which sapped my energy even more.

I managed to keep putting one foot in front of the other without too much trouble until the night came. With the night, came the fear. I was out in the desert in the middle of Jordan without anyone else in sight. It was dark and it was scary.

The race organisers were meant to have glow sticks every 500 metres or so to mark the way but they weren't always there and when they were they weren't always very visible. It would have been easy to get lost. I spent a lot of time peering into the darkness trying to find the next glowing stick. Every now and then, I'd lose sight of the glow sticks altogether and have to stop and check my compass for directions. It was scary. As the sun came up after the first night running, I was highly relieved. Even though it meant that the air would soon be hot, I didn't care. I wouldn't have to keep looking for those damned glow sticks!

A couple of times along the route, I met up with an older Austrian guy and we'd run together for a while. It was great to have company for a few hours before one or other of us would go off on our own.

The second day was a struggle to get through as the cumulative effect of exhaustion and the deep sand I was struggling to get through started to wear me down. By the afternoon we started to climb into the mountains passing small groups of huts along the way. Even though the terrain was firmer under foot, the fact that I was climbing all the time made it harder. The route peaked at 1500 metres above sea level.

Just as I started to conquer my fear of the dark on the second night, everything turned to custard. I lost the lights and I knew I should have been pretty close to a checkpoint but I just couldn't find the trail. It was so dark I couldn't use my compass. It turned out I'd gone a couple of kilometres off the track, which in itself was terrible as every step counted. While I was panicking about not being able to find the checkpoint, I realised that I was surrounded by a pack of wild desert dogs. It was absolutely terrifying. All I could do was keep moving. The dogs continued to circle me barking away for about 20 minutes until I finally found the checkpoint. To this day, I don't know why they didn't attack me.

When I got to the checkpoint I was beside myself. I grabbed the first human being I saw and wouldn't let go. He must have thought I was crazy. I had him by the shirt and was yelling, 'The dogs are after me, the dogs are after me! Don't make me go out there on my own again.'

The poor guy led me into the tent and managed to calm me down. He assured me that the dogs had gone and that I'd be quite safe. But I wasn't having a bar of it. There was no bloody way I was going out there on my own again so I decided to wait in the tent until the next runner came along. What do you know? Half an hour later my Austrian mate turned up. He took a break and we decided we'd run through the rest of the night together. I left that checkpoint a whole lot happier than when I'd arrived!

As we ran together we soon found that we were both struggling a bit so we coaxed each other along. Before long, my body was so completely challenged that I got dysentery. Sometimes it happens on these races that your body becomes so over-stressed that you just lose all control of normal functions. Unfortunately, this meant that we had to stop every few minutes for me to void my bowels. Even so, we stayed together and kept each other company.

After a while, we were holding hands comforting each other along the way. We must have looked like a couple of old drunks staggering along encouraging each other to continue. When one of us would flag a bit, the other would be all, 'Come on, mate, you can do it. You can finish this!' Without him, there was no way I could have finished that race.

The last kilometre into Petra was incredible. We came over a big hill and there, spread out below us, was this entire ancient city. I just wish I'd had more time to take it all in. The city is carved into the pale pink rock of the hillside. I was too shattered to appreciate the view and focused on getting to the end but at least I managed to appreciate the historic significance of that magnificent city. The two of us stopped next to one of the ancient temples and took a photograph before carrying on.

By the time I crossed the finish line I was in floods of tears of sheer relief. I'd done it. I'd completed the race in 46 hours and I was the tenth woman to finish. I was knackered. Sadly, while the rest of the competitors spent time recovering and exploring Petra, I spent the next day and a half in bed. I made it to the restaurant to eat every few hours and then I'd crawl back into bed, all the while being filmed by the documentary crew.

When I got back to Vienna, material from the documentary was shown on *Vera* as well as on a national breakfast show called *Welcome Austria*. It was fantastic that people were interested in what I was doing and it also meant that Coke kept financing my exploits. I was hooked on this ultra-running lark and since money was no longer quite so much of a worry I started to book myself into every race that I could find.

Home life over this time was becoming more and more strained. I was still with Werner but it was clear that our lives were heading in different directions. I was completely obsessed with ultra-running. My jewellery business also kept me busy — there was a well-established jeweller in Vienna selling my work in his shop. I loved the creativity that making jewellery offered me. It meant that I used a completely different set of skills from running. Between the two I felt really fulfilled — as if I was finally coming into my own.

Werner and I drifted apart. It was never a match made in heaven — he was a good man but we were in such different places in our lives. I was just getting into gear and he was ready to slow down and take it easier. Sport wasn't a priority and he was very overworked. Eventually we lived fairly separate lives.

Dealing with inflammation

Most of the pain and injuries that you get are caused by inflammation. In most of these cases, you're not really doing any damage to yourself by keeping going. If you have to, take anti-inflammatories but be careful with these as they can cause digestive issues. Anti-inflammatory sprays are also good for long distance running. It's great to have a good cold ice spray to help bring inflammation down.

Compression gear is really important when you've finished a race. When I finish a race I hop into a really cold bath or shower or, if needs be, the sea. This can be incredibly painful but it helps to stop your body from swelling and cools inflamed muscles. Once you've done that, get into your compression garments to further prevent swelling and inflammation. You'll be amazed how quickly your body recovers if you do these two things.

13

MORE MOROCCO

To achieve in life you need to lose fear

While the romance with Werner wasn't going well, everything else was great. Even before I got back from Jordan I knew that I wanted to do the Marathon des Sables again. With only five months to get ready I couldn't wait to get back to Morocco.

Having done the race once, I felt like a veteran. I knew exactly what to expect and I knew that I could improve on my time from the previous race. The only thing that would change was the route. Every year, the race takes place over a different route and you never know what it is until you get there. This prevents the locals from gaining any advantage from being able to train on the actual course — not that they need it. They usually win the race anyway!

The team I'd worked with in the build-up to the Desert Cup stayed with me in the months between coming back from Jordan and leaving for Morocco. I trained hard over those five months all the while becoming more professional in my approach to the race. It was great to be back with the Austrian–German team and there was a real excitement on the plane as we flew towards Casablanca. We all had dinner together two nights before the race while we waited for all the pre-race formalities to be completed. At that dinner I talked to Gerhard Lusskandl for the first time. He told me that this was his first ultramarathon and he wasn't sure what to expect. Being an old hand at it, I told him he'd be fine.

At the 5 kilometre point of the first stage, Gerhard ran past me and recognised me from the dinner a couple of nights earlier. He called out to me and asked me how I was going. He was running with a colleague of his who hadn't trained properly and he was holding Gerhard back. Knowing that I had a bit of experience, Gerhard asked if he could run with me. I thought about it and decided that if he didn't hold me back, there shouldn't be a problem.

As we ran we talked and at the end of the first day we realised that we'd kept a similar pace the whole day and that we had compelled each other to keep going at a good pace. At dinner, Gerhard and I talked about it and decided to meet up the next morning to run together the next day.

The second day went as smoothly as the first and we decided we'd do the whole race together. I found running with someone who is both really good looking and great to talk to was incredibly motivating. I was determined not to drop off the pace and lose touch with this lovely man. I guess I was showing off a wee bit, but I was determined to impress Gerhard.

This had one pretty serious drawback. It meant that I was in the top five women nearing the finish of the third day. If you're in the top five women or the top 50 men, you have to stay back three hours on the long fourth day. This was designed to stop the field from stretching out too much. Everyone is out on the course for so long that day, that if the fastest runners left at the same time as everyone else the field would become very split up making it harder to ensure that everyone is all right. It also provides a huge mental challenge to the leading runners as they end up starting the longest sector in the hottest part of the day.

As the fifth woman, I would have been the slowest of the fast group. I'd pretty much be running on my own and I knew I wasn't going to be able to keep up with the rest of the field. It also meant that I wouldn't be running with Gerhard, which was what had got me so high in the rankings in the first place. It would have been a disaster for me. The long stage on the fourth day is always brutal and we'd been running through sandstorms, which were forecast to continue. The route was also taking us through a whole lot of high sand dunes, which we'd have to run through while getting lashed by sand. There was only one thing for it. I dropped my pace back a bit on the third day to make sure one of the other women passed me. It's not something I would probably do now, but at that stage I knew it was the best thing for me if I was going to finish the race in a decent time and in reasonable health.

I finished day three in ninth and got to continue the race with Gerhard. Heading into the long day together was pretty scary and our fears were soon realised. The sandstorms were horrific and we had 40 kilometres of sand dunes ahead. The dunes made going incredibly difficult — as we got to the top of each one the windborne sand would hit us. It was like having a million needles flying into your body and you couldn't see a thing. Even with a hat down over my forehead, a mask over my mouth and nose and sunglasses on, the sand kept getting in my eyes.

Getting through the sand dunes was a slog. It wasn't helped that once we'd been trudging through the dunes for four or five hours, the front runners all went flying past us. They were unbelievable. It was almost impossible to believe that they were human, especially the two Moroccans, the Ahansal brothers, who between them win the race every year. Being born and bred in the desert clearly has its advantages.

Gerhard and I were desperate to be out of the sand dunes by night-fall. Once it got dark, we wouldn't have been able to see a thing and there would be a greater risk of getting lost. To help people orientate themselves through the dunes, the race organisers had projected a laser beam into the sky for runners to follow. The sand storm was so bad though that it was impossible to see the beam. We were both afraid of getting lost.

Risking dehydration and worse, we went like crazy to get out of the dunes before it got dark. Just as night fell we summitted the last dune and in celebratory mood we walked down onto the salt flats. We still had another 25 kilometres to go across a solid bed of salt while being lashed by the wind but we were out of the dunes and we'd made it through the worst that the race could throw at us.

Everyone carried emergency flares with them and we could see them flying into the sky left, right and centre behind us as we made our way across the salt. Because of the sand-laden wind, the race support helicopters were grounded and couldn't get in to rescue anyone.

The next day we heard that two Americans who were still in the dunes in the dark had got lost and it took the organisers nearly 24 hours to find them. By the time they were located, they were incredibly dehydrated but at least they were alive. It's an absolute miracle that no one died during that part of the race, the risks were huge.

Running across the salt plains, Gerhard and I would take turns at running in front of each other to create a slip stream in the wind for the other, like draughting in cycling. Before long, more runners began to take advantage of this and were running in single file behind us. Even though it's each for their own out there, I couldn't believe that hardly any of them would take their turn at leading the bunch. It was pretty much left to one other guy, Gerhard and I to do all the hard lead running.

Gerhard got a grain of sand under his contact lens and he could barely see a thing. One eye was completely blind and the other one only had a little vision in it. The damage to Gerhard's eyes was so severe that when he got back to Austria he had to have eye surgery to try to restore his sight. I don't know if all those other runners would have been quite so keen to follow us if they're realised that the lead guy couldn't see where he was going.

While Gerhard couldn't see, I was giving him directions. I'd yell left or right from behind him so that he could avoid any obstacles along the way and to help him follow the guide lights. Despite his sand blindness, we managed to complete that stage in 12 hours and 15 minutes and we were in the top 100 of the 700 runners.

Crossing the finish line we were holding hands and I gave Gerhard a big hug. And suddenly I knew. I knew that this man was going to be very significant in my life and I knew that with him at my side I could achieve anything. But that was all I knew. I knew nothing much about him.

I turned to him and all I could think of to say was, 'Who the hell are you?' We got talking and it turned out that he was a year younger than me and he worked as a police officer in a rural part of Austria. He had been married before and had two children but was divorced.

In the sand storm, my tent had been blown over and no one else on my team was back yet. I didn't have the energy to resurrect the tent on my own and Gerhard couldn't see it to help me. There was nothing for it but to go back to his tent. A couple of his teammates were there but we shared a meal — for which read a muesli bar, a handful of nuts and a drink. It was hardly your typical romantic first date, but it was a very intimate moment charged by having just survived an incredibly difficult experience together. There was no physical contact between us and there was nothing said but it was clear to me that there was a real connection between the two of us.

We were both so stoked that we'd made it through the worst day and we knew that we had the morning off the next day. This was because runners have 24 hours to complete the longest stage. The runners who complete it early all rest and wait for the rest of the field to come in.

For the next two days we continued to run together and I struggled like hell to keep up with Gerhard. He could have gone a lot faster but he made the decision to stay back and wait for me. Gerhard could have made a much faster time than he did but he put helping me ahead of his own goal. I was really impressed. It was such a change from being constantly derided and mocked by Paul. This guy was really impressive.

When we finally made it to the finish line, we went across it holding hands and with the Austrian flag aloft. I'd bettered my time by 15 hours. I was ecstatic. After we crossed the finish line neither of us would let go of each other's hand. Everyone was jumping around, thrilled to have completed the race. We were both grinning, too, but I think we both knew we had more reason than most to be feeling so happy. It wasn't until we went to get on the bus to go back to camp, still holding hands and hugging each other, that we finally had to face up to what was going on. This was the first time that we'd had any physical contact and it confirmed to me what I had suspected. I said to Gerhard, 'Umm, I think we might have a bit of a problem here'.

He wanted to know why. I felt sick having to tell him that I had a partner but I assured him that my relationship was all but over. I was terrified by what Gerhard's response would be and I couldn't believe it when he said, 'I've got a great big house in the country. When are you moving in?'

Reeling with joy and a little trepidation, I told him I'd be there as soon as I'd sorted things out with Werner.

14

GOALS AND GOATS

Become committed. It is never too late to start your life.

Werner was there to meet me at the airport when the team flew back into Vienna. It was one of the worst moments of my life. I knew without a doubt that we had to break up but I didn't want to hurt this man who had rescued me from the abuse I'd suffered in my previous relationship. Werner had been my saviour and I really wished that things could have been different.

I just couldn't tell him about Gerhard straight away but he must have suspected that something was wrong. I'd been home for two days before I gathered up enough courage to have a quiet moment with Werner and tell him that I'd met somebody while I was in Morocco and that I was leaving.

Werner's reaction was better than I could have expected. We had a bit of a cry together and agreed that we both hadn't been happy for a while. I packed the few possessions I had and left the house. It was surprisingly amicable between us.

I left Werner and Austria to come back to New Zealand for six weeks. I left the relationship with what I'd brought into it. There was no way I wanted to take anything from Werner after all he'd done for me. Despite the way our relationship ended, Werner and I stayed friends. Flying home, I couldn't help but worry what my family were going to say when I told them that my relationship with Werner was over. When I arrived, Mum and Dad's reactions came as a complete surprise.

Mum had been in Austria for a couple of months between my first Marathon des Sables and the Desert Cup. It turned out that she didn't think things were good between Werner and I at that stage and she wasn't happy that I was in a relationship that wasn't working. She knew that we didn't talk anymore and she saw that our lives were almost completely separate. Mum wasn't surprised when I told her we'd broken up. Dad's reaction was perhaps more surprising. He was stoked for me. I think he was pleased that I had had the courage to leave a relationship that clearly wasn't good for me.

Once I'd told them about Gerhard and about what a good man he was, they were really happy for me. Dad was delighted that I'd met someone who had the same interest as me and who would be able to both challenge and support me at the same time.

When I got back to Austria from New Zealand, I moved straight in with Gerhard. He lived in a village called Wantendorf, in Lower Austria. We were about an hour and a half out of Vienna — right out in the country. Gerhard had built the house and it was a lovely home. He had a huge section with a river running through it and I couldn't have wanted for anything more. Life was great but no matter how good life was I always had a hankering for New Plymouth.

Gerhard worked long hours for the police force and I tried to keep my jewellery apprenticeship going, commuting into Vienna each day. Spending three hours a day commuting was absolutely exhausting. It also meant that I didn't have as much time to train as I would have liked and Gerhard and I didn't have a lot of time together either. In the end I had to make a choice. I decided that my relationship with him was more important than completing my apprenticeship so I gave it up. But that wasn't to be the end of my jewellery career. Before long, I'd set up a studio at home and continued to design and make pieces. It was great fun to spend plenty of time honing my skills but I ended up with a load of jewellery and no way to sell it.

Pretty soon though, I had something else to fill my days. Not long after I moved in with Gerhard we had planned our lives together. It was pretty clear that we both wanted to get married and we decided to do it back in New Zealand. We waited for nearly a year. We wanted to spend the time getting to know each other. Life wasn't going to be like in the desert where we lived in an artificial reality. After living together for a while, we'd rubbed the corners off each other and we found that we were still very much in love.

Gerhard's mother couldn't stand me. The first time I met her she completely ignored me. I was gutted. His parents lived quite close to us and his father was incapacitated as a result of a stroke some years earlier. This meant that they relied on Gerhard and he spent a lot of time helping them out.

Coming from such a close family, I'd have hated it if he didn't spend time with his family. But Gerhard's mother was never going to accept me. It seemed as if she thought I was there to take his money — I couldn't have been less interested in his material assets. She hated having to share her baby with anybody. Gerhard was her youngest son and he was her baby, the apple of her eye. I found her incredibly dominating but Gerhard didn't seem to see it.

After a while, the relationship between Mrs Lusskandl and I seemed to thaw a bit but only until I'd dropped my barriers enough for her to get into our house and start telling me how to run my life. She used to come over and tell me what a terrible housewife I was and how I didn't do things in the proper Austrian way. I wasn't having a bar of her trying to tell me how to do things in my own home and I made that quite clear to her. It looks like Paul's auntie hadn't taught me the art of being an Austrian housewife quite as well as I thought! After that, it quickly turned to custard and she did her best to freeze me out of her life and her son's life.

In February 2003, 11 months after we first met, we flew back to New Zealand to get married. Gerhard told his parents he was coming to New Zealand on holiday to meet my family. He knew his mother would be furious if she found out we were planning to get married so he never mentioned it to her. It was sad that it had to be that way but we really felt we had no choice.

On the flipside, my parents couldn't wait to meet the man who'd turned my life upside–down. I was nervous about coming home with Gerhard but I needn't have been. Mum and Dad loved him and they could see how much I adored him.

Gerhard and Dad got on really well and before long, the pair of them were off hunting together. Dad decided that he'd give Gerhard a few tips on how to shoot a rifle, instructing him like he was a beginner. He was impressed when Gerhard hit every target. Dad told him that every shot had to be a head shot. He was pretty impressed when Gerhard managed to follow his instructions with ease. He got three big goats in no time. Dad was really impressed — what he had forgotten was that Gerhard was a policeman and a crack shot.

Dad joked that Gerhard had to prove himself before he'd give his approval for the pair of us to get married. He insisted that Gerhard prove his prowess by going out hunting with him and killing a pig. Despite all Dad's experience, the pair of them couldn't find a pig to kill so they had to settle for another big goat. Gerhard knocked it off no problems but to really prove himself, Dad made Gerhard cut its head off and bring it home for me. Who says diamonds are a girl's best friend? My man killed a goat for me — talk about romance!

Having spent all our time together on the other side of the world, I was a bit worried that Gerhard wouldn't like being in New Zealand. I needn't have worried. He loved the lifestyle and was really relaxed and happy while he was here.

In the weeks before our wedding, Gerhard and I made each other's wedding rings, which was a beautiful thing to be able to do for each other. They were difficult rings to make but once again Gerhard proved his ability to pick up new skills and he managed to work out how to make my ring really quickly.

The wedding was simple but perfect. We got married on the Ahuahu Road Beach with our friends and family. I was wearing a twenty dollar dress and carried a bouquet of wildflowers picked from the Taranaki roadside. Gerhard was wearing a Taranaki Hardcore T-shirt and shorts and he had bare feet. My cousin James was Gerhard's page boy and my little cousins, Jasmine and Emma, were our mermaids, instead of bridesmaids. It was a delightful and simple ceremony.

A friend of Dad's, a sea captain named Chaddy, was the celebrant. It was great to have someone who knew our family perform the service. At the end of our vows, Chaddy added in a promise that neither Gerhard or I knew about. He turned to Gerhard and said, 'Do you, Gerhard, promise to share your mountain bike with Lisa?' While Gerhard hadn't hesitated making any of the earlier vows, this was clearly a bit too much. He answered in a flash, 'No.'

It was a lovely romantic day that was all about the marriage rather than being all about the wedding. After the ceremony, everyone headed back to Mum and Dad's place at Oakura where we had a big feed of crayfish for dinner, heaps of singing and a cheeky drink or two. I couldn't have been happier. The only cloud over the day was that none of Gerhard's friends could be with us on our special day.

When I got back to Austria, Gerhard broke the news to his parents that we were married. His mother was very tight-lipped about our union. After that I felt like she did everything in her power to undermine me — she was determined to split us up. I don't think Gerhard could see that.

Despite that, Gerhard and I were really happy together. Our household revolved around training. Doing the Marathon des Sables in Morocco had hooked Gerhard on ultra-running, too, so our house was now home to two ultra-athletes.

Before we got married Gerhard and I had talked about moving to New Zealand one day, but the longer we spent in Austria, the more it seemed that this was not going to happen. If we settled in New Zealand, it would have taken Gerhard away from his parents who depended on him, his children from his previous marriage, from the house that he built and from the career that he'd made for himself. Even though I missed home desperately and longed to live in Taranaki near my own family, I did my best to build a new life in Austria with Gerhard.

For a start we'd train together but it soon became clear that

Gerhard was a superior athlete to me and he didn't need to train as much as I did. He was so much faster than me that training together was out of the question. Despite both of our busy schedules, Gerhard and I took part in as many races as we could. We spent most weekends travelling around Austria, Germany and other neighbouring countries competing in 12- and 24-hour races.

Our training programs meant that we didn't see that much of each other, but Gerhard found a way for us to spend heaps of time together — he decided that it would be great for us to do the 2003 Trans Europe Foot Race together. The plan was to run from Lisbon in Portugal to Moscow in Russia — a whopping 5100 kilometres — in 64 days.

It was a daunting prospect but having completed so many difficult races before, I had every confidence that we could do it. The training started in earnest and we began fundraising to cover our costs. Sadly, it was not to be. A few months before we were due to go on the race, Gerhard was out playing social football one weekend and was the recipient of a particularly rough tackle. A guy just slid into him and took his feet out from underneath him. He fell awkwardly and ended up with a badly broken leg.

The Trans Europe Race went ahead without us and, amazingly, 21 of the 49 starters managed to finish the event. It was such a tough race that it wasn't run again until 2009. One guy I talked to who completed the race claimed it had nearly turned him into an alcoholic. He said they didn't always have food at the end of a stage but there was always red wine — sometimes two bottles a day. The drink helped numb the pain and so he took it. It sounded absolutely atrocious.

When Gerhard came out of hospital, I was tasked with looking after him. Luckily I had some experience of nursing a man with a broken leg! Thankfully, Gerhard wasn't anywhere near as driven as Paul and he coped heaps better with being incapacitated. He's such a natural athlete that he didn't worry too much about not being able to train. However, it took Gerhard a couple of years before he could really run competitively again. Over that time I continued training as I don't like to miss a single day's training if I can possibly help it. Gerhard was really supportive of me over this period and he was happy to crew for me while I did shorter races around Austria, Germany and the Czech Republic.

When I found out that the 24-hour world championships were being held in the Czech Republic, I decided it'd be great if I could go and represent New Zealand. I made some enquiries and found out that New Zealand weren't sending a team. Seeing as it was just near where I lived, I offered to pay my own expenses to go. For a while it looked like I'd finally represent my country at an international meet. I don't know what happened but not long before I left to go to the meet, I got a message from New Zealand to say I wouldn't be able to compete under the Kiwi flag. I was really disappointed but decided to race in the open section anyway and had a great time.

Mum made another trip to Austria and I was so excited to see her. She was much happier visiting now she wasn't expected to bike everywhere. One classic moment of Mum's visit — that I'll never let her live down — was when I was showing her around the house. We were up in the attic and Mum turned around and said to me, 'Oooh, here's where you could hide from the Germans . . .' I just cracked up and turned around and said, 'Mum . . . we ARE the Germans!' It was absolutely hilarious. I loved it when Mum came over but her visits also served to remind me of how much I missed life in New Zealand

and my family. Despite the distance between us, we had grown closer and the time we had together was always quality time.

With Gerhard all but out of action, I scaled back my training a bit and spent more time making jewellery. By the end of 2003, I had a lot of stock so I had a stall at a Christmas market in Saint Polten, a city about 15 minutes away from where we lived. The market was a huge success and I sold heaps of jewellery. Gerhard could tell that I wanted to further my career and so together we took a risk and opened our Lisa Lusskandl Schmuckdesign — my very own jewellery shop in Saint Polten. It was great working in Saint Polten as it was about the size of New Plymouth and you soon got to know your regular customers. It wasn't long before the shop started to pay for itself. I was amazed at how successful it was.

Over time, though, I struggled to keep up with designing and making the jewellery and doing all the administration that the business required. It put a lot of pressure on Gerhard as he had to support me by doing a lot of the paperwork. He already worked really long hours and my business put a lot of demands on what time he had away from his job. It was really difficult for both of us and for the first time, there was some tension in our relationship. The day to day grind was tearing us apart.

15

SOCKS AND SHOES

----

*You can't always change a situation but you can change
your attitude towards it*

By the time Gerhard had completely recovered from his injury and
was back training he was race fit within weeks. I was pretty jealous
of his natural athleticism as I reckon if I'd had to take two years off
training it would take me about two years to get race fit again. For
him it just came back like he'd never been away.

Gerhard and I were both completely addicted to desert running
and when the chance came to run the Trans 333 desert race in Niger
I was totally into it. Gerhard wasn't so sure about it but I told him
there was no way that I was going to run across a desert in Africa
on my own. After a while I persuaded him it was going to be a great
project for us and he agreed that we should do the race together. It
was going to be a tough one so we threw ourselves into training hard
out for it.

Life was pretty quiet for me over this time. Gerhard worked really hard and he worked long hours. Life for me was like life for policemen's wives the world over. He'd work night shifts quite often and there was always a shadow of danger over what he did for a job. I didn't really worry about him though as Austria is a pretty safe place and we were in a more rural part of the country, so I knew he would be all right. With Gerhard working hard, my long hours at the shop, and us not training together much our lives didn't intersect much but we had a common goal in the Niger race so we weren't worried about the time spent apart. We were on a mission — and I love a mission in life.

One of the races we did as part of our preparation was the Isar Run, which took place in May 2006. It was a 338-kilometre race over five days along the banks of the Isar River, which runs through Austria and Germany. We ran 70 kilometres a day for five days and I made a terrible mistake on the first day that was to affect the rest of my race. It was such a dumb mistake. I tied my shoelaces too tight. I know, it sounds like such a simple thing but it made the whole race a real mission for me as I got terrible shin splints and massive swelling in my legs. To start with, I didn't know what had caused the pain and I felt like a complete dork when I found out it was my shoelaces. After two days running, one of the old hands who was doing the race with me told me what the problem was and he told me to cut my socks. I did and it made all the difference but the damage was already done. How dumb! But it wasn't just me — Gerhard had the same problem.

The Isar Run is another stage race so instead of racing the clock, like I did in the Desert Cup, here I was actually racing against other runners so I went as fast as I could over the stage. The faster you run in races like this, the more intensive the breakdown of the body is. I'd get up in the morning in complete agony and struggle to get out of bed. But I knew I had to go on. I never wanted to give in and I couldn't face the thought of failing. That's the biggest driver there is to get you out of bed and make you keep going. When I start something like this, I will finish it or die trying — that's the attitude I always take.

On the last day of the race, I woke up and all I could think was that I had eight more hours to go. Eight more hours and I would never have to do this again. That was the only way I could make myself carry on. There were two groups — the fast and the slow — and I was in the slow group. Gerhard was in the fast group so I went and saw him off. I was completely pathetic. I was crying from the pain and I didn't know how I was going to complete the race. It was the worst joint pain I'd ever experienced in a race. I've had all sorts of digestive, kidney, liver and back problems but this was nothing like any of those. The physical pain was the most intense that I've experienced. And all because I'd done something — that most kids learn how to do at about the age of four — wrong.

After overcoming all the mental and physical obstacles in front of me, I made it to the finish line. I hadn't made a good time but I made it. Gerhard was already there waiting for me when I got across the line. For the first time, I wasn't elated as I usually was after completing a run like that. I'd been in third place throughout the race but I got beaten into fourth on the last day. I was gutted. The competitive part of me was no longer happy with just finishing. I wanted to do well and I hadn't.

After a race like that, your whole body swells up as a reaction to the extreme pressure you put it under. Gerhard and I had both ballooned up and we had to get a train back to Vienna the following day. The pair of us sat in the train with our legs up on the seats in front of us. We were in complete agony the whole way and when we arrived in Vienna, I'm not sure how, we managed to get all our gear off the train. The time that we'd been sitting down had meant that we swelled up even more and it was a real struggle to hobble back to Gerhard's car carrying all our stuff.

When we finally got home — it was a slow drive given the physical state we were both in — I took to my bed for a couple of days and I went for three days without training. That was the longest I'd gone for years without at least doing a few k's on the bike or having a bit of a run. It was two weeks before I could walk properly again and I realised that our dream of doing the Trans Europe Race would probably have ended in tears. If I couldn't cope with five days of this kind of running, there's no way I could have done 5000 kilometres.

The Isar Run would have put most people off doing another ultramarathon but Gerhard and I were due to run across Niger in a couple of months, so we just had to get on with it. I reckon it must be a bit like childbirth, you know? At the time you think, never again, then after a while you decide you want another baby. It's like that with ultra-running. Once you recover from the shock and stress it puts on your body, you can't wait to get out there and do another run. Besides, you always learn something from every race. With each run, you get better at what you do because you're always learning what not to do as well as what to do. Every race I've run has made me feel a little bit more proud of myself, a little bit more confident and a little bit more capable of dealing with whatever the next race can throw at me.

Footwear

When you're buying shoes for competitive running you should always go to a shoe store that has gait and foot analysis. They'll be able to assess your running style and your feet and make sure you get the right shoes. Here are my tips for getting the best from your footwear:

➜ *If you're doing an ultra-race always get shoes that are bigger than what you normally wear. I wear shoes that are two sizes bigger than I'd usually have. This is because my feet will swell heaps over the long period of time that I'm running. A good tip is to start with your shoes loose and then loosen them up more as time goes on.*

➜ *Be really careful that your socks aren't too tight. Normal socks will be OK at normal temperatures but as you get hotter your legs swell and the top of your socks can cut off circulation to your feet. That can cause really bad problems in your shins and knees. If you find that your socks are getting too tight, cut the sock at the front of the foot. It'll open up and release the pressure but you'll still have the sock around your foot.*

➜ *Don't go for a race shoe. You have to get one that's really well cushioned. The longer you're running the less shock absorption your muscles and tendons will have so you really need to rely on your shoes to provide as much cushioning as possible.*

➜ *If possible, change your shoes if you are doing a long race. The shock absorbing capacity decreases after a while so putting on fresh shoes will lessen the shock on your body.*

COUSIN KIM, DIVORCE AND GOAT CURRY

*Failure is simply a result you did not want and
a valuable learning experience*

In June 2006, not long after I'd completed the Isar Run, black toenails
and all, I went to Bangkok with the jewellery business for three
weeks. The trip went well and I was feeling pretty buoyant on my
way home to Austria, unaware of the bombshell that was waiting for
me. Gerhard and I had been planning a long holiday in New Zealand
once we'd completed the Niger race. When I got off the plane, he told
me he wasn't coming. He said, 'You go. I'm staying here.'

I couldn't work it out. Why would he not want to come back to
New Zealand with me? What was going on? He couldn't explain why
he wouldn't come. I was really upset as I'd spent the last few years
living in Austria. I couldn't understand why he wouldn't come and
spend even a few weeks with me at home.

While I'd been in Bangkok there'd been a huge change in Gerhard.

He'd been crewing for another ultra-athlete while I was away and he spent heaps of time with that crew and something obviously changed. A few weeks later we were both supposed to go and crew for another athlete on a race through France and again, Gerhard told me he didn't want me to go. I wondered whether it was because I'd just been in Bangkok for three weeks and I hadn't been working. I decided I could use the time to make sure things were still ticking over at the shop so off he went on his own.

I knew that he was under a lot of pressure at work and I thought that when that was resolved our relationship would improve. But his work issues were compounded by the fact that I had expanded my business to include a wholesaling arm.

When he came back from France, nothing I could do was right. Gerhard was really uncommunicative and didn't seem to want to be around me. A couple of weeks later, I was at my wit's end over my declining relationship with Gerhard, when my cousin, Kim, and her partner, Neville, came to stay with us for a couple of months. I was stoked to have Kim with me — we are more like sisters than cousins. It was also really cool to have some of my New Zealand family here and I was really excited about showing them Austria.

They'd only been at the house for a couple of days when Gerhard came to me and said, 'I think we need to have a break. Things aren't working out so I think we need to go our separate ways for a while.' It completely blew me out of the water. I had no idea that he was even contemplating splitting up with me; I just thought we were having a bit of a rough patch and we'd work things out. We had both been under a lot of pressure at work and this had a knock-on effect on our relationship but I didn't really think that things had got this bad.

I was lucky to have Kim there to help pick up the pieces. She was my rock during that time. With just a week to go before we were due to leave for Niger and a 333-kilometre desert run, I was gutted. We'd been training for the Niger run for a year and a half and this was not ideal finish to our preparation.

I kept trying to talk to Gerhard before we left for Niger but didn't get anywhere. In the end, we agreed that we'd put off dealing with everything until we got back from the race. I had no choice but to go to Niger with Gerhard. I knew that I couldn't do the race on my own and all our preparation for the race had been on the basis that we'd do it together, but Gerhard had changed his mind. I was going to have to run the race on my own trying to ignore the fact that my life was falling apart. It was hell.

We flew down to Agadez in a plane full of aid workers as they seemed to be the only people who ever went to Niger. After spending several hours going through all the Customs processes, we were picked up by race organisers. I thought that the large entrance fee we'd paid to run the race might have stretched to a hotel bed, but apparently not. They took us to a restaurant that was little more than a tumbledown hut. We all had dinner there and then we ended up sleeping on some open ground outside the 'restaurant'. The next day we piled into a jeep and drove for two days into the desert to reach the start line. Here I was stuck in a jeep for hours on end, heading for one of the world's hardest races, with a man I completely adored who had just told me he didn't want to be with me. I can't imagine a more miserable scenario.

The start for the race was at a spot called the 'Tree of Tenere'. Only it wasn't a tree. It was a metal post where the locals said there used to be a tree — the only one in this part of the Sahara. The locals said it had been run over by a truck. I'd be surprised as there wasn't any vegetation for miles around. We spent a night at the Tree of Tenere getting organised for the run. I thought the race was going to be organised like the Marathon des Sables had been. I know there were only nineteen runners but the organisation was terrible. The guy that organised the race had got so many things wrong I barely know where to start.

The organiser had assured us that there'd be safe food supplies brought in from France for the runners and their crews for the days leading up to the race. There wasn't. Other runners had obviously heard about how chaotic these races can be and they had brought their own freeze-dried food. Stupidly, I hadn't. I only had the food that I'd need for the race and I couldn't risk digging into those supplies before I really needed them.

The night before the race, I had the choice of not eating anything or eating a goat stew that some locals had made. Gerhard never really ate before races so he had vitamin drinks. But there was no way I could face starting a 333-kilometre race across the Tenere desert on an empty stomach so goat stew it was. And boy did I come to regret that decision.

The next morning, I woke up at about six o'clock. It was still quite cool and it took me a moment to work out where I was. Then it dawned on me. I was in the middle of the Tenere desert and there was no way out but to run. 'Oh shit,' I thought. 'Whose stupid idea was this?' The Tenere desert is a mean bit of the Sahara that stretches through north eastern Niger into western Chad. Temperatures during the day reach into the forties and at night it plunges into the low single digits.

Despite the fact I'd been training for this for a couple of years, I was feeling in less than tip-top condition. To be honest, I felt scared.

I got out of my sleeping bag and did a double-check of my gear. So we knew where to go, we had a set of handwritten co-ordinates and a GPS. Carrying the GPS meant that I had to take heaps of batteries along with the rest of my gear.

By seven o'clock the butterflies in my stomach were going hard out. I tried to convince myself it was the fear and not something a lot lot worse. Lining up at the start line, I said goodbye to Gerhard as he'd decided to try for a placing and I was just focused on completing the race. There are two races within one, the Trans 222 and the Trans 333. Both are non-stop races and there were fourteen checkpoints along the way. To make managing the race a bit easier, the organisers had set time limits for runners. We had 36 hours to run the first 111 kilometres and 108 hours to complete the whole 333 kilometres. I was determined to finish the 333-kilometre race.

At 7.30 am, the nineteen of us lined up at the start. There were 17 men and 2 women. The gun fired and we were underway. Gerhard goes out fast and I watch my husband disappear off into the distance. I was going to have to get used to not having him around so I might as well start here.

There was a howling wind blowing sand straight in our faces and the terrain was flat deep sand. It's hard going dragging each foot out of the sand to put it down in front of the other. We'd been told to expect 110 kilometres of that before we would be moving into rocky terrain. I decided that I'd better get used to it fast — having to drag myself through sand for a third of the race.

The whole time we were in the desert it was really windy and we needed to follow GPS co-ordinates to stay on course. Even though my backpack for this race was lighter than it had been for any of my past desert races, it felt heavy right from the start. I was carrying everything I needed for the next few days running — I had some food, some water, a sleeping bag, a first aid kit and some spare clothes. I knew we'd be given water at the checkpoints but the organisation was so bad that there wasn't even enough water at some of the checkpoints.

Only an hour into the race, the butterflies in my stomach were still there only they'd turned into something much less benign. My guts were in uproar and I know that it was far too early in the race to be dealing with dysentery. Still, I took some solace in the fact that I wasn't the only one dropping to the side with alarming regularity. After the race, I found out that four other runners and two of the support crew who had all shared the goat curry I'd eaten the night before had come down with food poisoning. We had all had to tough it out throughout the race. Now, that's one elite group of athletes I could live without being part of!

After so much training, effort and cost, to have a race affected so badly by something as simple as a dodgy meal was heartbreaking. At that moment, I could have happily strangled the race organiser but I also knew that I was as much to blame for not having taken the precaution of bringing my own food even though we'd been told that the food would all come from France. Soon enough, I realised that I'd just have to work regular toilet stops into my race plan and that I'd need to ration my water intake slightly differently to make up for the fluids that I was losing. I just tried to keep on running — I had to face hundreds of kilometres of desert with a terrible bout of food poisoning and a divorce hanging over my head. Great! Shot, Lisa. I really knew how to make life hard for myself.

While most people would climb into bed and pull the duvet over their head and hide from the world, I had no choice but to continue running. There was no way out but to keep running forward. Quitting and going back with the crew would mean failure, and there was no way that I was going to let that happen. I knew that if I gave up in the middle of the Niger Desert, I'd probably never recover.

The other female runner was an English woman called Eleanor. Pretty soon we fell into step together and it was nice to have company out there in the middle of nowhere. Eleanor was not one of the unfortunate few who'd bonded over the goat stew so she was in a much better condition than me. I was so very grateful for her positive attitude and her encouragement while we were out on the course. While I was with her, I was pretty much running blind. She held my hand and I just followed her. I kept collapsing and Eleanor kept picking me up and urging me to carry on.

Throughout the first day, my stomach was cramping badly and the intensity of the cramps grew with every passing kilometre. I tried my best to ignore the pain and just keep running and it worked while the sun was out, but as soon as night fell I realised just how much trouble I was in. The dysentery had become extreme and I felt like I was spending more time shitting than I was running. I made it past checkpoint two and got some more water but checkpoint three felt like a long, long way away.

Apart from other runners and race officials, the only other people I saw out in the desert were men who were transporting salt across the desert in big trucks. We'd been told that it was only safe to sleep at checkpoints because if you slept out in the desert there was the possibility of being run over by one of those trucks. Whenever I came across a truck, the men would stop and stare at me. They couldn't work out what the hell I was doing out in the desert. They'd ask where I was going and I'd tell them I was running to Agadez.

They couldn't believe it. 'All the way to Agadez, running? But you'll die. You'll die! We'll take you.' I assured them all I was OK and that I'd make it to Agadez. They'd drive off into the desert shaking their heads at the crazy western woman.

Before I made it to the third checkpoint, I completely hit the wall. My blood sugars had bottomed out — please excuse the pun — and I was horrendously dehydrated. Even though I'd been drinking plenty of water, no sooner had I put it in than it would come straight back out again. I was in a real state. The one positive thing was that the camaraderie between the runners in this race was brilliant. Eleanor did her best to keep me moving forward. I kept collapsing and she kept picking me up and putting me back on my feet. With two kilometres to go to the third checkpoint, I collapsed again. At this point, two other runners came past and they both lifted me out of the sand and practically carried me to the checkpoint. By the time I got there, I had collapsed four times that night.

At each checkpoint along the way, and there were fourteen of them across the 333 kilometres, the medical team would wait for the runners to come in. The doctor took one look at me and handed me some tablets to take to try and stop the dysentery. I gulped them down willing to try anything that might get me out of this predicament. The doctor also recommended that I rest for an hour or two. I lay down and tried to sleep for a while but the stomach cramps kept me awake.

Half an hour after we'd arrived at the checkpoint, Eleanor decided she was ready to keep moving. I was terrified of being out in the desert at night on my own so I dragged myself out of the medic's tent and went with her. I'll never know where I found the strength to keep running that night but when the next day dawned, I had 95 kilometres of sand behind me. When I made it to the fourth checkpoint, someone told me that Gerhard was up with the race leaders and that he was looking really strong. I was happy for him and it gave me a bit of lift. Despite everything, it helped me to carry on.

By the time the sun was high in the sky, the temperature was soaring. At midday, it was 45°C and we were still making our way through deep sand. When would this bloody sand end? With the sun burning down and the relentless wind hurling sand into my face, I felt dreadful. The medication I'd been given for the dysentery had worked for a while but before long the dreaded symptoms returned and I was still suffering the effects of the dehydration it had caused. My body was struggling to retain the water it needed and food was pretty much out of the question. The equation became quite simple — no fuel equals no energy. I knew that my body would be burning fat and muscle instead of nutrients but I had to keep going. Of all the races I'd ever done, this was definitely the hardest. I knew it would be hard but I hadn't counted on the break-up of my marriage the week before and the onset of food poisoning on day one.

News filtered through to me that three of the other runners who ate the stew had pulled out of the race. I felt terrible for them but most of all I felt scared that I'd be next. The whole time I was calculating in my head, am I going to make it in time? How many kilometres will I have to do before I can rest again? I knew I was still within the time limits the race organisers had set but I wasn't sure how much further I could go. My body was screaming at me to rest but I knew only too well that each hour I rested, meant I was an hour further from completing the race.

Eleanor decided she couldn't wait for me any longer and continued the race on her own. I completely understood her thinking. I was so sick I was holding her back. I wished her the best and off she went. By the third night I'd passed checkpoint nine but was having to stop every 20 minutes to empty my bowels — the dysentery was back with a vengeance and I was still nearly 150 kilometres from the end of the longer course. At checkpoint ten, I was given more medication for my dysentery but it was only 22 kilometres until the end of the Trans 222 race and I had a big decision to make. Did I stop at the final checkpoint for the Trans 222 or did I continue on and risk having my result being recorded as a 'did not finish' in the Trans 333 race.

Eventually after three days and nights of some fantastic highs — the beautiful landscape and the camaraderie between runners — and the worst lows, I decided that my run would end at the finish line of the Trans 222 race. Before I left for Niger, Mum had made me promise not to kill myself doing the race. I could hear her voice in my mind and I knew that by continuing I would be seriously risking my health. I had to stop.

I had desperately wanted to complete the longer race and I tried to convince myself that I should be happy with completing the 222, but I couldn't. Even though I'd done my best, I'd failed. I'd just gone through the hardest 62 hours of my life and I'd failed to do what I'd set out to do.

Still, I was relieved when I climbed into my sleeping bag at the end of the race and went to sleep. Once I'd had some time to recover, I caught a lift to the finish line of the Trans 333 with some of the race organisers. I joined the cameraman who was making a documentary about Gerhard's race and followed the last 10 kilometres of his race. Out here in the desert, it just didn't seem real that our life together in Austria was in the process of falling apart.

Gerhard was running with an English athlete called Mark

Cockbain. They'd teamed up quite a wee way back and they were pacing each other. They were both in a pretty bad way. They hadn't had enough water and were incoherent. Thankfully, they'd made a pact to finish together so they egged each other along. While 10 kilometres doesn't sound like much, they were going at a slow crawl and it took ages before we made it to Agadez. The combination of having failed to complete my race, seeing Gerhard's condition and thinking about what lay ahead for us meant that I was in tears the whole way.

Agadez is a huge city but it's incredibly poor. As Gerhard and Mark made their way through the dusty streets of the town, kids surrounded them. They gave away everything they could to these kids who had absolutely nothing and as they reached the finish line in the city of Agadez, they made sure to cross the finish line together. They were second equal having completed the run in a time of 81 hours and 34 minutes. I was so proud of Gerhard.

Gerhard and I spent a couple of days in Agadez before we went home. The whole time we didn't discuss what was going on. It was impossible — we were being followed everywhere by a film crew who thought that everything was fine.

Jack Denness, an ultra-running legend, had been there before and he took us to a local school. We took all our leftover muesli bars, sweets and anything that we thought the kids would like with us. We also had a whole lot of pens for them, but the pens weren't that useful because the school was little more than a concrete shelter, with no desks, chairs, blackboards or, indeed, paper. The kids were all crowding around us so the teachers ushered us into one of the classrooms and blocked the door so that the kids couldn't get in. We thought that the teachers would let the kids in one by one to divide the stuff out. But, no . . . To our surprise, the teachers started hooking into the food themselves! Any of the kids that tried to get in the room were dealt a hiding by the teachers and we just couldn't believe it. Despite having spent a lot of time in third world countries, the extreme poverty in Niger still shocked me.

I also visited a silversmiths' in Agadez. The workshop was incredibly basic. The jewellers sat outside in the dirt with their anvils in the ground, using hammers and nails and saws, yet they were able to make incredible pieces of silverware. It was all beautifully handcrafted and so intricate. I was really impressed by what they could make with so little — I even learned a technique or two from them. I bought as many pieces as I could afford and treasure them to this day.

Food

The chance of getting stomach problems in many countries is substantial but if the following simple rules are followed the chances will be drastically reduced:

1) *Only eat foods you can cook or peel.*

2) *Only drink bottled water.*

3) *Stay away from salads and other food that has been washed.*

4) *Carry dysentery medication with you at all times.*

5) *No matter how tempting they look, don't eat local ice creams.*

6) *If you're racing in a third world country, make sure you take your own food with you if you're not sure about the race organisers*

COMING HOME

Happiness does not lie in whether or not you have problems but
in the way you handle them

Returning home to Austria, I had hoped that things between Gerhard and I would be able to be sorted out. I shut down the wholesaling part of my business to try and alleviate some of the pressure, but it was too late. Gerhard told me he wanted to continue the separation and that I should go home and see my family as I'd planned. At that stage, the trip was to be for two months at the end of which I'd come back to Austria and we'd reassess our situation. Nothing I said or did could change his mind.

It was already November and I had to stay in Austria for Christmas as it was the busiest time of year for my shop. Whatever else was going on, there was no way I wanted my business to fail the way my marriage had. Christmas is such a huge deal in Europe. Everyone buys heaps of presents and traditions are very closely followed. Something like 40 per cent of my annual turnover came in the few weeks before Christmas, so everything in the business was geared for the madness of that month.

I closed the shop on Christmas Eve. Kim and Neville had left a few days before so I spent Christmas with Gerhard's family. Christmas in Austria goes for several days and it was a pretty tough time for me but it was either spend Christmas with them or spend it on my own. No one mentioned the fact that I was leaving and we all just pretended that nothing was wrong.

On 29 December, I flew out of Vienna and by New Year's Eve I was at home in New Plymouth with my family. I had always dreamed of moving back to New Zealand but I never ever thought it would be like this — I always thought that it would be with Gerhard and I'd be happy. Here I was, on a trial separation from the man I adored and feeling miserable. Happy 2007, Lisa!

Two weeks later, despite Gerhard's assurances that this was just a trial separation and that we just needed some time apart, the divorce papers arrived in the post. It was like being smacked in the head. I felt like he'd manipulated the whole situation to make sure I left the country so he didn't have to face me and hand me those papers himself. Despite everything, I was pleased to be back in New Zealand and I knew there was nothing for it but to set about rebuilding my life. Mum had opened a shop in New Plymouth selling my jewellery and Dad's paintings about 18 months earlier so I went to work with her. She was really tolerant of me coming in and rearranging the shop and together we built the business up as much as we could. I bought into an opal-cutting business, which gave me another avenue to pursue in the jewellery world and got on with life.

After six months, I knew I had to go back to Austria to tie up all the loose ends I'd left there. It was hellish being in Austria as I was still hoping that Gerhard would change his mind.

The shop was doing really badly because the manager wasn't looking after it properly. When I got back everything looked terrible and I knew I had to sell the shop. Unsurprisingly, the manager indicated that she was interested in buying it and I sold it to her at a loss. She had made sure that the value of the place had dropped so low that she could afford to buy me out. In the end, I walked away having cleared my debts, and refunded Gerhard some of his investment. All I had to show for the years of business was my pieces of designer jewellery and some of the other stock that I'd built up.

It was difficult to leave Gerhard, but I walked away from my life in Austria knowing that my future lay in New Zealand. I was happy to be going back to live with my family, friends and my own culture. Having spent six months at home already, my self-confidence had started to come back and I was beginning to get things back on track.

When I got home I threw myself into the opal business that I'd invested in. I was passionate about working with opals and I revelled in the beauty that Taranaki has to offer and I tried to make the most of being there. Over that time, I was talking to Gerhard on a regular basis always trying to convince him to change his mind. If he'd said the word, I'd have got on the next plane out leaving everything behind once again but it wasn't to be.

I still had a hankering for more athletic pursuits. I was training but I felt as if I needed to be around people a bit more. In September, I tripped over while I was out running and broke my arm. I couldn't go out and train on the roads for a while so I decided I'd better join a gym. I signed on at City Fitness in New Plymouth.

One of the first people I met there was Chris Cruikshank, who worked as a personal trainer. He was curious about the chick training with a cast on her arm and we got talking. We got on like a house on fire. He really made me laugh but he also managed to push me to train harder and get better at what I do. The rest of the team there were fantastic, too. Anyway, as Chris and I trained together, I talked to him about the races I'd already done and one day he asked me if there was any ultra-race I hadn't done that I wanted to do. There was only one possible answer to that question — Badwater.

I told him that I didn't think it would be do-able because of the cost and he wouldn't hear a word of it. From that moment on, Chris was determined that I would run the Badwater Marathon. He didn't know when or how, but he knew it would happen. I was stoked to have a project to train for and focus on. Together we went through the application process. Every year there are about 900 applicants and only the 80 most-qualified are accepted to do the race. Gerhard had run Badwater the year before and I had more experience ultra-running than he had so I was pretty confident that I'd get in.

I'd already started raising money while my application was being processed but it wasn't until I had the acceptance letter in my hand that I really believed that I was going to do the race. The day I got that letter was really exciting and it was all on from there. Once again, I was excited at the prospect of getting back out into the desert.

Chris talked to his boss, Neil Wagstaff, about our plan. He was on board straight away and he helped us with the fundraising side of things. Before long, the spare room at Neil and and his wife Sam's house was Death Valley Central. All the gear that I was going to need gradually took over the beds and pacing charts adorned the walls.

Their commitment to helping me complete the race was incredible.

I had met Sandy Barwick a few times and she was my idol — I knew I had to have her on board. She agreed straight away. The core of Team Tamati was born and Neil, Chris and Sandy were all there with me every step of the way. Sometimes, they were literally with me on training runs from New Plymouth to Opunake through the night on Fridays. Chris and Neil would take turns to run with me over the 62 kilometres while the other one would drive the crew vehicle. We'd get to Opunake in the middle of the night then turn around and drive back to New Plymouth, arriving back in town just as other people were heading home from a night out.

We also used the mountain for training. The three of us would park up next to Egmont Village and run up the mountain. The only way to get back to the car was to run back again so there was no pulling out!

The gym

I never believed in going to the gym until I started training for Death Valley. I trained so hard, I didn't think I needed to do any more indoors. I thought that I just needed to have fit legs, I didn't think my upper body needed working out, but I was wrong.

What I've learned since training with Chris and Gerard Fynmore (aka Fyn) is that the body needs to be balanced. Posture when you're running is hugely important and it involves the entire body. Your upper body will pull your body back and your lower body will pull your body down. All your muscles are there to support your spine, by supporting your spine, you support your ribs. By supporting your ribs, you support your lungs. And what's a runner without good lungs?

When you're training it's important that you're working with a trainer — but make sure that they're well qualified and that they know what your goals are. They'll provide another set of eyes and be able to work with you to improve not only your fitness but also your approach to training and racing. A good trainer will focus not only on training but also on recovery. You'll get the best results when you balance your training and your recovery.

CHIP BUTTIES AND PUMPKIN SOUP MAN

Do not be content with half measures for halfway is as close
to the bottom as it is to the top

Up until now I'd never competed in New Zealand. I'd done all my ultramarathons in the desert or in Europe. It was time to throw myself into the Kiwi scene and see how I measured up. One of the first races I decided to compete in was the 2007 24 Hour National Championships. They were due to be held at the Sovereign Stadium on Auckland's North Shore on 12 October.

The championships are organised by the Sri Chinmoy Marathon Team. The team organise ultra-running races all over the world and have been real pioneers in the sport of ultramarathons. They organise the races on the principle of self-transcendence, which basically means that runners should compete against themselves rather than other runners in order to gain greater insights into themselves.

Sri Chinmoy, who was the motivating force behind the

organisation, was an Indian philosopher and spiritual teacher. He was famous for holding public events around the world on the themes of world harmony and inner peace. He taught many people to meditate and always preached tolerance and love.

Sadly, the day before the race on 11 October 2007, Sri Chinmoy passed away. Naturally his followers, mourning their leader's death, cancelled the race just hours before it was due to start. I had arrived in Auckland the day before with my support team — Mum, Cousin James and Dad's mate, Greg Edley — in tow. I had trained hard and was amped to get running when I got a message from Sandy Barwick to say the race had been cancelled. I was gutted to hear the news. I also felt badly for the Sri Chinmoy Marathon Team.

As the news sank in, I had an idea. I decided that I'd do the run anyway. It wouldn't be an official race but I just wanted to get out there and run. I hoped that it wouldn't offend any of the organisers but I felt pretty sure that Sri Chinmoy would have approved of me taking on the race all by myself. It turned out that I wasn't the only one thinking that way and when I got to the track there were a motley bunch of people ready to run, regardless. The weather was terrible and the rain was absolutely chucking it down but that didn't put us off.

There were quite a few people aiming for the 6- and 12-hour runs. There were only two of us attempting the 24-hour run — me and Macca, aka Alex McKenzie. It was his first attempt at anything longer than a marathon so I wasn't sure how he'd go, but Macca is a physical trainer in the New Zealand Army and he's hard as nails and crazy with it. It was my first experience of running with Mad Macca but it wasn't the last!

One of the great things about having Macca there was his support crew — he'd brought a whole pile of his army mates with him. They pitched their tents and they were more than happy to help out the rest of the runners with food, shelter and tons of encouragement. They really got stuck into the role that the race organisers would have. I had Mum, James and Greg there to look after me and cheer me on. I'd asked Greg to make a really simple pumpkin soup for me. It's a great source of nutrition while you're running. Greg had kind of missed the bit about using a simple recipe and he'd made 5 litres of pumpkin soup full of garlic, onion, ginger, orange and honey. For some people this might be a gourmet treat, but it wasn't so good for me going into a whole day and night running around a track!

As the runners gathered together at the start, we had a moment of silence for Sri Chinmoy. Then, Gary Regtien and Sandy Barwick started us off, giving the gathering some semblance of actually being a race. So, unofficial as it was, we were off.

Macca and I kind of fell into running together because we were both planning to do the 24-hour race. We got talking along the way and found we had a lot in common. Macca's dry sense of humour and his good pace meant that I ran really well for the first few hours. Because this was Macca's first ultramarathon, he hung back with me uncertain of how he was going to go over the longer distance.

For the first 10 hours or so everything went pretty smoothly. A lot of the other runners achieved the goals they'd set for themselves and completed their races. As the day drew to a close, the number of people out on the track gradually thinned. Throughout the day, Macca's crew, including his partner Dianne, had tirelessly recorded every lap that we ran and provided unstinting moral support for all the runners. It was awesome just having them there.

At around 7.30 that night though everything turned to custard

— or should I say mud. A wee cyclone had decided to hit Auckland and before long we were running through torrential rain and 100 kilometre per hour winds — just what we needed after the next 11 hours on our feet.

At the 12-hour mark, Sandy came out to run with us for a while. She said, 'You guys know this is unofficial. Have you considered calling it a day? You've done 12 hours and that's pretty impressive.'

Macca and I both thought about it for a minute and we both looked at Sandy and said, 'Nah. We'll keep going thanks.' Poor Sandy. I'm sure she'd have much rather been at home than watching two nutters plodding around a track. The same can probably be said for both of our support crews. They were all freezing their arses off in the middle of a muddy paddock but they were prepared to hang in there for as long as we were.

I've always been blessed with a huge amount of support from everyone around me when I'm running. I probably don't say it often enough but I really appreciate everything they do for me and I try and remember to thank them for every little bit of their help and support.

By 9 pm, there was only me and Macca out there on the track in the howling wind and pouring rain. Even though we were both knackered, I still managed a good laugh when Macca turned to me in all seriousness and said, 'Lise, if we're not careful, before long we'll be doing a duathlon'. It took me a while to work out what he meant but then he started doing this weird swimming motion and I got it! The track was almost under water.

It was raining so much that no matter how much of Greg's pumpkin soup got drunk, there seemed to be more. Every time anyone braved a cup of it, the rain would top the pot up! At one point, I'd had enough of the soup so I asked my cousin James to get me a slice of bread. James ran back to the tent and told the guys I wanted some bread. Everybody in the tent was eating chips so some smart aleck decided to put some chips in my bread. James duly delivered the tasty sandwich to me. I don't think he'd ever heard me swear before and he was a bit shocked to hear me say, 'Don't give me that crap. I just want some f**king bread!' I was too spaced out to realise I could have chucked the chips away and just eaten the bread.

Things were bleak but we kept plodding along. Macca had long since wiped out his personal distance record and I was hoping to do the same. I wanted, at the very least, to reach the 160-kilometre mark. Just when I was starting to think I wasn't going to make it, Nick Linton appeared out of the rain like an angel. He offered to run with us for a while and it was great. As much as I was enjoying running with Macca it was nice to have someone else to run with for a while. Nick also ran back and forth supplying us with food and drink. He was great.

We had a break at midnight to get a quick massage and to try and eat some real food. In the shelter of the freezing cold army tent, hypothermia was starting to set in not only on me and Macca but on some of our crew. Mum told me after that she'd never felt so unglamorous and unprepared before in all her life. James was hanging in there and Greg was braving the weather out on the track in his old Swanndri jacket.

Despite the hideous weather, my support crew still urged me on. Mind you, if any of them had complained, I would have pointed out that Macca was so determined to do his personal best that he wouldn't even stop for a pee. He'd just run and pee. Thank God it was raining. What did this have to do with his crew? Well, it was them that were massaging him when we stopped. Gross, yes, but that's the world of ultra-running!

It was good to have a break but I just wanted to get back out on the track. The more I moved, the warmer I stayed. However, I was having trouble eating. This had been an ongoing problem whenever I raced, but since joining the gym and getting my team of Death Valley trainers together we'd been sorting it out. Macca had no such problems. At one stage, Nick asked him if he wanted a sandwich. Macca said he did. Nick's response, 'What do you want? We've got jam, banana, Marmite, peanut butter . . .' Macca said, 'Yeah.' Nick was a bit confused, 'Well, which one do you want?' Macca's response was 'All of it!' I swear that man could eat road-kill!

It wasn't long before I realised that hypothermia was starting to affect me. At one point, I felt myself just slip out of consciousness briefly. As I fell, Nick Linton caught me. That combined with dehydration and digestive issues meant that after 18 hours and 15 minutes, I finally decided to call it a day. Well, not quite a day but near enough. In the end I'd covered 135 kilometres. I'd really wanted to reach my goal of 160 kilometres even though it wasn't an official race.

Macca managed to carry on for another two hours before also deciding to chuck it in. I still reckon he could have finished the whole 24 hours if he hadn't been worried about the state of his crew. Even though it had turned out to be nothing more than a pretty extreme training run, I was really happy that I'd decided to run. It was great to meet Mad Macca and to make a whole pile of other new friends. Best of all, it felt good to be running at that level in New Zealand.

Nutrition

In general, you'll get more out of good organic raw food than the processed stuff. I try to eat a good balanced diet when I'm training but when I'm running it's a different story.

If a race is longer than 10 hours, I can't eat anything solid. My digestion shuts down but I still need to take in calories and energy. In those cases, I rely on drinks like Sustagen, which is easily digestible and contains energy, protein, vitamins and minerals. I also have electrolyte drinks, bananas and flat ginger ale while I'm running. Small sips of flat ginger ale settle my stomach, the sugar provides a boost and it tastes great. Make sure it's flat though — the bubbles will cause no end of trouble in your stomach if you're running.

Any drink you take should be lukewarm. If your body is running hot and you drink something that's 5–10° colder than you are, it will shock your system. If it's too hot, it'll have the same effect.

19

MAD MACCA AND THE MUPPETS

We become what we think about

About six weeks later I met up with my new mate Macca again for another one of New Zealand's famous ultra-races. This one was a little bit closer to home for me — the Around the Mountain race in Taranaki. This race is run by relay teams of between ten and sixteen members but there's a few of us hardy souls who run the whole thing. All up, there are 22 legs over the 150–kilometre course.

The race starts in New Plymouth, passes through Inglewood, Stratford, Eltham, Opunake, Pungarehu and Oakura before arriving back in New Plymouth to complete the circumnavigation of the mountain. The 2007 race was due to start at 9 pm on 30 November at the race course in New Plymouth. I'd assumed — incorrectly, as it turned out — that it would start and finish at the same place. I was hanging out at the finish line getting ready to run and I couldn't work out why no one else was there. At about 8.50 pm I realised my mistake and ran over to the start line, getting there with just a minute to spare!

Macca was going to be doing the race with me so we decided to share a crew van. All his gear was in with my stuff and to make it to the finish line in one piece we really needed to stick together. Macca wasn't having any of it. Once we got going out of New Plymouth, Macca, the big expert having run one ultramarathon, decided I was too slow and he took off. Hadn't anyone in the army taught him it was plain dumb to cut yourself off from your supply lines?

I carried on racing the way I'd planned. I knew I wasn't going to be on my own the whole way anyway — I'd convinced my trainers to run with me for some of it. Neil was going to do the first 40 kilometres with me and Chris and Nick planned to run with me on and off over the final 70 kilometres.

While I was training for this race, Neil and Chris had decided to finally try and solve the issue I had with not being able to eat while I was running. So, this time they pumped me full of food in the early parts of the race, when I normally don't feel like eating. It was a bit of a risk, but it worked a treat. My energy levels stayed high and I felt pretty good. But I was getting a bit worried about what I was hearing had happened to Macca.

I'd managed to run right through the night and Dad came out to see how I was getting on. On the way, he'd seen Macca weaving all over the road, crying and completely out of it. He'd had hardly any food or drink the whole time he'd been out there and he'd hit the wall. Dad grabbed all Macca's gear out of our support car and he and Greg, the pumpkin soup guy, went off to help Macca. Poor Macca having the Muppets — old school rugby players my dad Cyril and his mate Greg — to support him!

Of my parents, Mum is the one that's spent more on the sidelines while I've been running and she knows exactly what runners need when they start to cramp and she can tell when they need a rest break. Dad and Greg had their own ideas. Macca was cramping badly so they chucked him down on the ground on top of Greg's Swanndri and hooked into his legs with a big jar of liniment. It might have worked with the boys when they were playing rugby, but it wasn't so great for a tough fella that has just run through the night and whose legs are full of lactic acid. Macca must have been in agony — the poor bugger was barely conscious and here were these two Muppets giving him a deep-tissue massage with burning liniment.

According to Dad, Macca kept asking for his special weapon after that. Dad was a bit worried as he knew that Macca was an army boy — surely the massaging hadn't been THAT bad. But no, it turned out his special weapon was chocolate-coated coffee beans. Macca reckoned the combination of caffeine and sugar was just what he needed to give him a bit of a boost out on the road. Dad had to confess that he'd seen them in the car and, thinking they were peanuts, he'd tried one. When he got a mouthful of grit, he decided that they'd gone off and biffed them out the window. Macca was gutted.

Greg decided to make it right and went into the next pub along the way and asked for a handful of coffee beans. Poor Macca, he ended up eating some bitter-as-hell coffee beans instead of his favourite chocolate-coated treats. Dad laughed as he reported that Macca looked like some sort of swamp monster dribbling dark, gritty water!

Because of Greg's efforts, Macca managed to win the race. OK, there were only three of us but credit due, Macca came in first. He was stuffed. Crossing the finish line he was bawling his eyes out and he hit the ground. Dad and Greg picked him up and held him up as long as it took for the photographers to capture the moment. It must have been hilarious.

Meanwhile, I was quite a way behind Macca. Neil ran with me for the first 42 kilometres and over that time we really got to know each other. It's amazing the things that you find interesting and entertaining while you're out on the road. After Neil finished his run, Chris and Nick took turns running with me and keeping me amused. During the early morning hours I started to feel a bit low. It was cold and there was still such a long way to go. Up ahead of me, the support van slowed and as I came up alongside the door opened and Nick jumped out wearing only a G-string. He started running along in front of me. That really lifted my spirits! Driving past at the same time was a van load of heart- and lung-transplant patients who were doing the relay race as the Beaters and Breathers team. I was pretty relieved that the sight of Nick's bare arse in the Taranaki moonlight didn't cause any of them to have relapses.

It was a great run for me. I had a fantastic support team and I felt really good. In the morning my brothers joined me on the run into Okato. It was the first time they'd come out to see what I do and I think it really gave them an insight into just how hard my sport really is. When we got to Okato I got the monster massage from Chris, Nick, Mitchell and Dawson. It must have looked hilarious seeing all these burly men massaging little old me on a mattress on the side of the road. Dawson ran 12 kilometres with me and Mitchell ran a half marathon. It was great to have them by my side.

As we ran into Oakura, it felt like the whole town was out cheering me on. It was an amazing feeling. All up Chris ran about 70 kilometres with me and in the last 15 kilometres from Oakura he was more gone than me. Where he was usually looking after me,

I spent most of the way into town trying to convince Chris that we were heading in the right direction. He was determined that the race was finishing at a rugby ground and it was all I could do to persuade him we had to go to the race course!

Having escorted Macca to the finish line, the Muppets — aka Dad 'n' Greg — decided they'd escort me to the finish line. I ran across the line with Chris, Nick, Dad and Greg. The rest of the crew were all there waiting for me. This was the first time I'd run a race like this at home in Taranaki and I'd had heaps of support from family and friends. It was absolutely awesome.

After I finished the race, one of my crew members decided the quickest way for me to get in cold water was to get me into the sea. I was completely exhausted and the water was freezing. Getting in was painful to my ultra-sensitive body. The waves were rolling in and out, I could hardly stand up and I couldn't stop crying. I was shaking, but my crew wouldn't let me get out of the water. Several people came over to find out what was going on as they thought that I was being abused. It was a bit embarrassing but good to know that Taranaki people were looking out for me. It was worthwhile — my recovery was amazingly fast.

Pain

Pain is a response to inflammation of the body. When you're doing something like an ultramarathon there are three types of pain, listed in order of severity:

➜   *Superficial pain, like chaffing and blistering.*

➜   *Deep throbbing pain caused by deeper inflammation.*

➜   *Systemic pain from things like torn muscles and broken bones.*

It's really important to be able to identify the difference between these three types of pain. The first two can be worked through. Don't be a tough arse and try running through the third type of pain as it's likely to cause long-term damage if you do.

From a training perspective, you want to reduce the pain, or delay the onset of pain, as much as possible. Superficial pain can be eased with sticking plasters and the like. That deeper pain is slightly trickier to deal with. It can be caused through joint inflammation and muscle seizing. When this sort of pain hits during a race, doing some stretches to ease the muscles and taking in food to up the energy levels can help. Every person can tolerate different levels of pain and people will process it differently.

When to intervene

If you're crewing for someone and they're talking or they're crying, then that's good. You know that they're in touch with what's going on. It's when they switch off completely, become unresponsive and just keep plodding along that things are getting a bit more risky. If that happens think about pulling the athlete back and encouraging them to take things a bit easier.

TEAM TAMATI GETS UNDERWAY

If you shine the spotlight on your strengths, you will excel

Training for Death Valley was pretty tough. I ran the 100 kilometre nationals even though I'd injured my back quite badly falling off a chair at the shop. I was in agony the day before the race but, somehow, I managed to drag myself out there and do the run. Even with the injury I got second.

I also did heaps of time at the gym and running around Taranaki. To try and get used to the heat I'd put on heaps of clothes when I was training. Another thing I did to try and prepare me for Death Valley was train in a sauna. I'd get in there and do step-ups and that sort of thing. I did that two or three times a week to try and get used to the heat. The key with heat training is to avoid overdoing it and depleting all your mineral reserves before you get into the desert. The only real way of getting used to the heat is to spend time in the place where you're going to run. Unfortunately, I had a long way to go before I could afford to take my team over to the United States.

Neil, his wife Sam, Chris and I had a meeting at City Fitness and we brainstormed about how we could get the money together. We invited Andrea Needham to the meeting as well. We'd met Andrea on the Around the Mountain Relay as she was one of that amazing team of heart- and lung-transplant survivors that had enjoyed Nick's impromptu strip show. We knew that she was an expert on leadership so we decided we'd ask her for some advice.

Once I'd explained to her what I wanted to do, she just got it straightaway. From that moment on she took over the project management and the fundraising for the project. She was unstoppable. Her energy and dedication was awe inspiring. Andrea recommended that we set up a trust and she got lawyers and accountants on board. Luckily, Andrea knew the right people to ask and soon Govett Quilliam, lawyers, and Staples Rodway, an accounting firm, were on as sponsors.

Andrea's networking skills were incredible. She went to work trying to raise sponsorship, asking everyone she knew and she quickly found my principle sponsor. Andrea belonged to a group of women who all had businesses that enabled them to work from home. They met once a week so that their working lives didn't become too isolating. It also gave them a forum to talk about any issues they had with their businesses. Inge Naenen-Vercammen was a member of the group. Inge and her husband, Marcel, had moved to Taranaki from Belgium in 1999. Soon after, they set up their own business, Van Dyck Fine Foods, making crepes, blinis and hotcakes.

Andrea told Inge about my plans to run through Death Valley and how I needed a naming-rights sponsor. Straightaway, Inge said, 'Yep, we'll do that'. On the spot she agreed to pay a lot of money to be my principal sponsor. Inge then had to go home and tell her husband what she'd done. I can't imagine he was too thrilled that she'd committed a large portion of their marketing budget for the year! Despite any reservations Marcel might have had, they were true to Inge's word and very soon we'd signed a contract with them. From there things really snowballed. Now that we had our main sponsor, other companies were happy to come on board. Taranaki people were amazing. It didn't hurt that my brother Dawson had played rugby for Taranaki and people knew that I was 'Dawson's sister'!

One person that Dawson put me onto was David Casey. He's the owner of local company, Big Media, who specialise in billboard advertising. David listened to my story over a wine one night. Straightaway he was keen and said he was happy to do whatever he could to help, including tapping some of his contacts for cash. David rang his mate at Crave Club, the local strip bar, and they chipped in a pile of money. David also decided that I needed more exposure — thankfully not the type that you'd see in the Crave Club — and he gave me space on two huge billboards in prime spots around New Plymouth to let people know what I was doing.

Blank billboards weren't going to be much use so Fire Design joined the team and came up with some awesome graphics for the billboards. The feedback from these boards was awesome. Heaps of people approached me wanting to know what I was doing and how they could help. The buzz was building and, before long, the local newspaper was onto my plans. They'd report whenever I did another race and they'd print updates about how my preparation and training was going.

Once the papers were reporting about the project, radio stations started to get interested. City Fitness did a lot of advertising with

More FM so it seemed natural for them to sponsor me, too. They gave me a huge advertising budget and they backed me up 100 per cent.

With the City Fitness guys we held a 12-hour endurance day at the gym. Members of the gym and local people came in and would run with me while I did 12 hours on the treadmill. Gerhard even joined me on the treadmill. We'd kept in touch since our divorce and he really wanted to come back to New Zealand to see me and spend some more time here. We had a great time together and he helped me with my training. Gerhard had run Badwater in 2007 so when he offered to crew for me, I jumped at the chance. After everything we'd been through, he knew me better than anyone and his experience would be a huge benefit to the whole team in the States.

Over the endurance day at City Fitness, heaps of people came in and ran with me, many of them doing personal bests, which was cool. It was so great to be able to meet, run with and thank people for their support. Maori TV covered the day and that helped to get the message out to the rest of New Zealand. That day Andrea's home business group came out in force, too. They went out on the streets of New Plymouth and rattled buckets to collect donations. They were absolutely amazing.

Sandwich Extreme, a sandwich shop around the corner from our shop, came up with a really novel way of supporting me. They put a Lisa Tamati sandwich on their menu — it was a really healthy combo of salmon and cottage cheese so it fitted the cause nicely. One dollar from every one of those sandwiches sold went towards my race fund. Every dollar we made was a step towards making it to Death Valley.

I really felt like the whole of New Plymouth and Taranaki were supporting me. I don't know if I'd have got that amount of support and excitement about what I was planning to do if I lived anywhere else in the country. Somehow, I'd managed to capture the community's imagination and everyone had faith in me and that I could do it.

I realised we needed to do a big event to raise awareness and, of course, cash. We decided to hold a night of entertainment and have an auction. I talked to the mayor of New Plymouth, Peter Tennant, and he offered me the use of a function room at the Devon Hotel, which he owns. It was so cool to have the mayor on my team!

I never do things by half, so I decided to have a fashion show as well as an auction. I managed to rustle up clothes from local stores and a whole lot of my mates to model them. We had to practice three nights a week to get it together but it was loads of fun and we were on a mission. It was hard work but it was a great night.

My cousin, Glen Osbourne, came down from Auckland and he emceed the night. He was fantastic. I can't believe what a hilarious speaker he is. He also managed to hold the whole show together. My other cousin, Hemi Takarua, played guitar and sang. We're a talented family, eh?

One of the highlights of the night was having the chance to help one of my friends fulfil one of the things on her bucket list. On her list of things to do before she died was to get her kit off in public. This was the perfect opportunity. To the sound of 'You can leave your hat on', me and two of my girlfriends — who shall remain nameless — and Chris, Hemi and Haden did a slinky striptease. It was hilarious. Thankfully, we didn't have to get nude. It was as tasteful as it could be!

Once that was over and everyone had had enough to drink we held the auction. One of the local real estate agents, Sandi Smith, was on hand to be the auctioneer. Sandi was amazing and she certainly managed to extract cash from people's pockets. As lot after lot went under the hammer, I got more and more excited. By the end of the night we had raised $10,000 by auctioning all the goods donated by local businesses. One of the best things was a beautiful painting my father had done of Mt Taranaki. It sold for $3500 — I was thrilled.

Once the auction was over, I knew that I was going to get to Death Valley. My dream was going to come true all because of the generosity and enthusiasm of the people of Taranaki.

Goal-setting

People say to me, you can run a couple of hundred kilometres so running a marathon must be easy. That's a load of rubbish. Whatever you set your mind to do on any particular day is what you've set out to do. You won't achieve any more because you've already decided on your goal. It's the same for me. If I set out to run 20 kilometres and then someone says do another twenty, I won't be able to. I'm shattered having finished the first lot. I have to prepare inside my head before going into a 200-kilometre race. I know what I'm getting in for and that's what I focus my mental preparation on.

No run is easy but whatever you put your mind to you can do. Ultramarathon running is about the top three inches. It's about setting goals and deciding not to give up before those goals have been achieved. That might sound easy, but it's not — especially if you're running long distances. Then there are hours and hours that you spend having to convince yourself to go on. You need to be really focused and know how much you're willing to sacrifice and how much you can put yourself through to reach your goal.

VEGAS BABY!

Seek out those who will challenge you.

The week before I left for Death Valley, the media interest was intense as we packed and double-checked all our gear. The feeling as Neil, Chris and I got on the plane to fly to Los Angeles was one of total relief. There'd been so much to arrange and do that we were all knackered. We could barely believe that we'd made it. We sat on the plane looking at each other almost in shock. But we were excited, too. We arrived in Los Angeles and headed down to Las Vegas. We had 10 days before the race — heaps of time to get over the jet lag, acclimatise to the temperatures and to relax a little bit after the chaos of the previous ten months.

The three of us tumbled off the plane in Vegas and we were like little kids. It was the Fourth of July and we were in Vegas. Yeah. As soon as we got off the plane, I was surprised to see that there were poker machines even in the airport. It was crazy!

As we were grabbing our luggage off the conveyer belt, I bent down to pick something up and accidentally banged my tooth. I must have banged it pretty hard because it fell out. Great. And to make things worse it was one of my front teeth. I couldn't risk running through the desert with raw nerves in my mouth. Never mind the fact I was about to meet the doco team from TVNZ's *20/20* looking like a pirate!

Outside the airport, there were lines and lines of limos and stretch Hummers and weird, Disneyland cars. I said to Chris, 'You wouldn't see that in New Plymouth!' We felt a bit like the country kids come to town. We picked up our much more modest rental car and headed for our hotel. We'd decided to stay in the Luxor. It's famous for its Egyptian theme and giant pyramid. The place was so huge we had to queue for nearly an hour just to check in!

Once we'd finally got hold of our room keys it took us about 20 minutes to walk to our rooms — Chris and Neil had a room together and I had one to myself. By this time it was about five in the evening and there were already heaps of people in the casino. Many of them were scantily clad women in heels like I'd never seen before. I reckon they had more plastic in their bodies than they did in their wallets! The boys loved it though and it didn't take long before they started playing a game they called 'real or fake'.

After we got to our rooms, our first mission was to find a dentist. That's probably not a strong priority for many people who arrive for a stay at the Luxor! Thank goodness Andrea had insisted on us taking out travel insurance. Once we'd found someone who'd fix my tooth the next day, we all decided to go for a walk along the Strip. It was going off — the whole street was crammed with people and there were all sorts of Fourth of July fireworks competing with the everyday garish neon of Las Vegas's main gambling road.

The thing that surprised me most was how quiet it was out there. I'd imagined that Vegas would be really noisy but it was a warm evening and the atmosphere was calm. Plus, it was completely surreal that we were finally there. We had quite a late night as there was just so much to see and take in. Eventually, the combination of the long flight and the Vegas heat meant that I was exhausted. When I got to bed I slept really well.

The next morning, we headed out to the dentist. It was the most high-tech dentist's office I'd ever seen. They even had massage chairs to sit in while you were waiting to see the dentist. The boys were quite happy sitting in their massage chairs watching the giant telly in the waiting room! Any relaxation benefit I got from the chairs disappeared once I was in the dentist's chair. The diagnosis was bad — I needed a root canal and a crown. I got the tooth fixed temporarily so I didn't have to worry about it while I was doing the race.

The next couple of days were taken up with going around the supermarkets, buying all our supplies. We needed a quarter of a ton of water, cool boxes, spray cans, dietary supplements, you name it. Every night we went out to a different restaurant in a different casino. We ate ourselves absolutely stupid because we could. The casinos all offer very cheap dining to attract people into their establishments to gamble. It was great for us as we ate the cheap food and didn't bother with the gambling!

We ate heaps and we continued training. While we were in Las Vegas we went running every day. The first day I took off down the strip with my face covered to protect it from the sun. Neil and Chris were with me and people on the Strip just stared at us. Most of them had gone there to have a great time and there we were running in 40°C heat. You see a lot of weird stuff in Vegas but one of the most bizarre things we saw as we were running down the Strip at about 11 o'clock one morning was a woman in a gorgeous wedding dress and all the hair and make-up. She was sitting there by herself drinking a yard glass of what looked like a Margarita. We could only imagine what her story must have been!

After half an hour of running in the heat, we'd head back to the Luxor absolutely shattered. Back in our hotel rooms, the first thing we'd do was switch the air conditioning off in an attempt to try and acclimatise a bit better to the heat. It was so tough I started to wonder what I'd got us into. But having Chris and Neil there with me made it much easier. We got on so well and we all egged each other on.

On the Friday, Gerhard and Sandy arrived — Sandy from New Zealand and Gerhard from Austria. As soon as they got there, we left Las Vegas and headed straight out into Death Valley.

Heat acclimatisation

When planning for a desert run or trek, it's always a good idea to acclimatise yourself to the heat. In his book, The Law of Running, *Tim Noakes says from you should be fully acclimatised to exercising in the heat after between 7 and 14 days. Over that time Noakes recommends that you should gradually increase the period you exercise over that period. He also says that any exercise in the heat that causes your body temperature to rise progressively, such as saunas, will help with heat acclimatisation.*

INTO THE VALLEY OF DEATH

You are not known by what you dare to dream but rather by what you dare to do

The further away from Las Vegas we got, the hotter it got. We drove past a sign saying 'Welcome to Death Valley'. I decided I wanted a photo of me standing in front of it so Neil stopped the car. As I scooted back to the sign, and after only about 30 seconds out of the car, I was roasting. I yelled at Chris to hurry up and take the photo because I was boiling. And I was going to have to run in this!

When we finally arrived at Furnace Creek — the base for all the runners in the race — at eight that night, the temperature was still in the forties. It was crazy. Furnace Creek also has the dubious claim to fame of being home to the hottest and lowest golf course in the United States. When I saw the sign proclaiming that I looked at Chris and asked, '*Why* would anyone want to come to Death Valley to play golf?' It just seemed so insane. Chris, not surprisingly, looked at me as if it was me that was insane and said, 'Lise, *why* would anyone come to Death Valley to run 200 kilometres?' Hole in one to Chris.

We rocked up to the arranged accommodation only to find that the motel had mucked up our booking and all five of us were going to have to share one tiny room. We managed — Neil, Chris, Sandy, Gerhard and me — to get ourselves and all our gear jammed into the room only to find the air conditioning didn't work.

It wasn't an ideal start to my first visit to Death Valley. Thank God we had another couple of nights before the race was due to start. By the second night, the motel people had managed to find us another room so Gerhard and I moved out of camp headquarters. Unfortunately our room was right at the other side of the compound and it took about 15 minutes to get from one room to the other. In the heat, that was enough exertion to leave us feeling exhausted.

Sandy became camp mother and she did the job really well. She was constantly doing washing and making sure all our gear was sorted. While she was doing that, Gerhard, Neil and Chris spent ages getting the team car sorted out. Everything needs to be easily accessible so packing the support vehicle really is a fine art. It wasn't long before I realised what a well-organised team I had compared to the other rookies in the race. Even so, the guys nearly had an own-goal when they left the 250 litres of water that we'd bought in the car. They hadn't been inside the motel long before they decided to go and check that everything in the car was OK and found that, in the extreme heat, some of the plastic bottles had already started to buckle. They carried all the water indoors to avoid a big wet disaster in the car.

On the first day, the film crew from *20/20* joined us so I spent quite a bit of time with them doing pre-race interviews. We also made a reconnaissance trip out to the starting point of the race at about 1 pm on the first day we were there. It was about 55°C when we got out there and I was petrified. The guys suggested that I do a training run while I was out there so I ran for 5 kilometres and I was relieved to find I coped OK with it. But Chris and Neil were absolutely poked. I reckon Chris only managed about a kilometre before crawling back to the car and going to sleep. The good thing about the training run was that it helped us work out a few glitches in our systems before the race began.

While we were out there, some American tourists came along in their car. They were shocked to see us running along the road. The guy wound down his window and the first words out of his mouth were, 'Are you guys craaaazy? You're gonna die out here. You can't run in Death Valley.' I told him I was preparing for a race through the valley starting on Monday but he wasn't having it.

'You're gonna die out there. Get in the car before you die.' When I wouldn't get in the car he drove off shaking his head. Thankfully, I didn't think too much about his predictions of doom because there's absolutely nothing you can do before you get there to prepare yourself for that kind of heat. All that time I'd spent in saunas had nothing on this.

The next night, just two nights before the start of the race, a huge storm came through. It's a really rare occurrence out there so we went out and found a good viewing-point to watch it roll through. It was beautiful. Even stranger, it was actually raining in Death Valley, where they get only a few millimetres a year.

The next day I woke up in a filthy mood and there was nothing anyone could do about it. I was freaking out and I was sick of the waiting. It was probably nerves, but there's not really any excuse for the way I behaved that day. Just as well the crew were amazing about it. I guess they realised the kind of pressure I was feeling or maybe they were just too scared to say anything!

Sandy, with the wisdom of experience, took me aside and said, 'Lise, let me tell you about my experience from doing these races. Two days out, I was always a mess. I was always freaking out and I always felt the most pressure on that day. Tomorrow you'll wake up and you'll be fine. You'll be calm and the adrenaline will start to kick in. Right now is the worst time you're going through. It's the two day out blues.'

Then Sandy gave me a massage and continued to calm me down. Not for the first time, I felt so blessed to have the legend that is Sandy Barwick on my team. She's run more miles than any other New Zealand woman and she's one of the few people in the country who has experienced the kind of extremes that I have. Thank God, Sandy was right. The next morning I woke up and I was calm and felt at peace. I was still scared but I was ready to take whatever Death Valley had to throw at me.

That day I had to attend a briefing with all the other runners. It was so exciting to be in the hall with all of my fellow competitors — some were my heroes. The race director went through all the race rules. He laid down the law to the media about what they were and were not allowed to do throughout the race.

Once that was over, all of the runners were called to the stage one by one and presented with printed T-shirts that said 'Don's Team'. Don was a runner who had done the race the year before and he was dying of cancer. We all put the T-shirts on for a mass photograph and it was then sent to Don by email. It sure helped take my mind off what I was facing over the next couple of days. That kind of thing really helps put things into perspective.

After that we all went and had our individual photos taken for the website. The race site was amazing — it was possible for anyone anywhere in the world to follow each runner online. Once the official photos had been taken I decided I wanted some of my own. Like a real fan, I asked Dean Karnazes and David Goggins if they would let me have my photo taken with each of them. They were both really great about it. In all of those photos I'm grinning ear to ear. I was at the most prestigious event in ultra-running and I was with my heroes. I was determined to make the most of it because I knew what lay ahead of me.

That last night before the race I managed to sleep better than I thought I would. I was in bed at 8.30 and Gerhard sat with me and went through everything that we'd done to prepare the team. That made me feel much better. He assured me I was going to be fine and I figured he, more than anyone, would know that was true.

The next morning, the alarm went off. I woke up and got moving really slowly. Even then I knew I had to conserve my energy for the race. I went off to get some breakfast and for some reason, I had my heart set on having French toast. I put some on my plate and Neil saw me. 'Uh uh,' he said. 'You're not having that.' I was furious and I made sure Neil knew it. I completely chucked my toys and stormed back to the room having had no breakfast. I knew that he was right because there was no way I should have been eating protein right before the race, but I didn't care.

I climbed back into bed in a complete paddy. I wouldn't move, wouldn't talk to anybody and there was only a couple of hours before I had to be at the start line of the race of my life. Finally, I managed to calm down enough to eat a banana.

Once the car was ready to go, Gerhard came in and helped me with my final preparations. He plaited my hair and made sure I had plenty of sunscreen on. He was brilliant. He did everything for me that morning. I didn't have to do anything. He was looking after me and I knew I would be fine. I was focusing 100 per cent on the race ahead. I was just pleased he was there and that he would be by my side throughout the next couple of days.

Eventually everything was sorted and we all piled into the car. The team were pretty quiet — it was probably partly that they were focusing on what they needed to do over the next few days and partly because Neil had told them about the French toast incident!

We got out to the start line about an hour before the race start-time and the heat was blistering. There were speeches and formalities to get through before the race finally started. Chris Kostman, the race director, gave a wee pep talk, the cameras were rolling, including those from the *20/20* crew that had come from New Zealand to film me. We were off — 84 competitors, including 22 women, with a 217-kilometre course to be completed in 60 hours.

After the gun went off to start our group, I went out really slowly. I was really focused on doing as little as possible to get that forward motion. I knew I had to keep moving forward and keep my pace slow. It took me about 5 kilometres to find my pace and my rhythm. Those first few kilometres are horrible. Like most, my body takes at least that amount of time to adjust before I slowly get into the rhythm of running. Until I've got my body up to operating temperature, it's horrible, but once that's reached I feel as if I have hit my stride and can begin to feel comfortable running.

During that first period of the race, I really just wanted to concentrate on my running, but I was surrounded by a bunch of over-excited elite athletes. They were all yarning away and talking about how many times they'd done the race and how great they were and I was freaking out.

There was one other female athlete in that group and she spent the whole time trying to mess with my head. She told me that I'd gone out too fast and that I'd pay for it later on. I thought I'd paced it pretty well but nevertheless started to worry. What made it worse was that during the first 35 kilometres of the race your crew aren't allowed to run with you. They were alongside, spraying me with water and giving me encouragement but I was running on my own. Those first 10 hours were the hottest of the whole race, too.

Between the heat and the mind games, I wasn't in the best of states. Of course, because of the advice I'd been given I was really worried about my pace and my speed. The guys in the car kept reassuring me that I was doing fine and after a while I had no choice but to believe them. By the 20-kilometre mark, I'd got away from the rowdy athletes and started to feel as if things were starting to go well. I kept looking over at Gerhard and he gave me heaps of encouragement.

At checkpoint one at Furnace Creek, I met up with my old mate Death Valley Jack — Jack Denness. The guy is a total legend. He's run Badwater 11 times and in 2005 he became the first 70 year old to complete the race. Since then Jack has worked as a volunteer on the run and it helps to have such a gentleman and hero around. I'd met Jack on the Trans 333 in Niger and we've been mates ever since.

It was an absolute pleasure to see Jack's smiling face there at the checkpoint waiting for me. I gave him a big hug and he told me I was looking good. He added, 'You New Zealanders are all tough. You've got the All Blacks over there and they're tough, too.' I couldn't help but laugh that even out here I was being compared to the rugby boys, and favourably, too!

The hottest 28 kilometres were now behind me and even better, from the first checkpoint on, our crew members were allowed to run with us. As soon as he was able Gerhard joined me as a pacer. With Gerhard at my side, I felt really strong. His experience of the race and the fact that he knew my strengths and weaknesses as an athlete made him the perfect running partner during the early stages.

The way the crew works on races like this is that there's usually one member running with me as a pacer. The other two will be in the vehicle — one of them driving and the other one either organising drinks, supplements, ice and stuff for me, or trying to get some sleep. The driver crawls along keeping about a kilometre ahead of me. When required, the driver stops the car, get outs and the support person hands out drinks and stuff to the driver. When I am about 100 metres away, the driver runs towards me and, when we meet, he turns to run with me. Then they give me whatever I need before returning to the car to get ahead of me once again.

At about the 30-kilometre mark, I went through a checkpoint as normal. For some reason my check-in was recorded but not uploaded to the race website and, all over Taranaki, people who were following the race online were worried that something had happened to me. More than a few people have since told me that they were really relieved to see my name pop up at the next checkpoint along the route.

After about 50 kilometres, the heat started to really take its toll. The entire race is run on the road so you're not just dealing with air temperature but the heat that's coming up off the road as well. Sometimes the road surface can get up to 90° Celsius. It was hot enough to fry an egg on as the documentary team from *20/20* proved! I ran on the white line down the middle of the road as much as I could because it was a bit cooler than the tarmac and it helped to stop my feet from getting cooked.

I knew I had to get through the hottest part of the valley as quickly as possible — most people who drop out of the race do so during the first 70 kilometres and usually because they're suffering from heatstroke. The lore of the race says that if you make it up the first pass, which is at about the 100-kilometre mark, then your chances of finishing are really good.

As I was battling the heat to get through the first 70 kilometres, my crew were battling serious problems of their own. Around the 60-kilometre mark the support car got a flat tyre. While most cars in New Zealand have the spare tyre in the boot, this American car had its spare tyre underneath the chassis encased in a plastic casing, but to get it out they had to unload the whole car to get to a clip that was inside the car! Neil and Chris struggled desperately to get the tyre out while feeling overwhelmed by the extreme heat coming off the road.

To make sure that the temporary absence of the crew vehicle didn't register with me, Sandy grabbed as much ice and food as she could carry and Gerhard stocked up on water and the pair of them ran on beside me. While a flat tyre is a pain at the best of times, in a race like this losing your support vehicle for any length of time can make the difference between finishing or not. The car carried everything I needed to complete the race and while Sandy and Gerhard did their best, they all knew that if they couldn't get the car fixed quickly my race could be over.

Meanwhile out on the course, I started to wonder why I hadn't seen the car for a while. Gerhard told me to concentrate on running and that Chris and Neil would be back soon. And he turned out to be right — thank goodness. The boys managed to get the space-saver tyre out and get the car back on the road fairly smartly under the circumstances. Everyone was just praying that the space-saver would last the distance.

My worries weren't over once the car was back on the road. Looking ahead, I could see the sky was blackening. The one thing we were pretty sure we wouldn't have to contend with in Death Valley was rain. We were wrong. The sky ahead brightened with flashes of lightning and thunder boomed around the valley. The average rainfall in Death Valley is about four centimetres a year and I reckon that much fell over the next couple of hours.

Going through a checkpoint, I was told that the road ahead had been blocked by landslides and flooding. This isn't unusual when it rains in the desert as sand doesn't soak up water very quickly. Even short periods of heavy rain can cause flood conditions very quickly and with little warning. As a result, what are usually dry ditches can turn into raging torrents and any area of low-lying land can turn into a lake almost without warning. As a result of the flooding, we were told that the route of the race would be changed to avoid the worst of the storm damage. I was gutted at the prospect of my first Badwater not being on the traditional race route. Thankfully, the flooding subsided almost as quickly as it arrived and within a couple of checkpoints I was given the great news that the original route had been reinstated.

I was still feeling pretty good so took a short break at Stovepipe Wells, which is a village with little more than a petrol station, a motel and a general store. While I was there the crew gave me a quick massage, a drink of Sustagen, and they did their best to patch up the holes that had started to appear in the skin on my back. I'd been looking forward to that stop for about 12 hours, but after the flat tyre and the hasty repacking of the gear, the crew vehicle was in chaos and it wasn't quite the smoothly run pit stop I'd looked forward to.

Not long after my stop at Stovepipe Wells, just as the sun was starting to set, I passed the magic 70-kilometre mark. It had taken me just over eight hours, averaging about 8.5 kilometres an hour. But there was no time for celebrating as ahead of me lay the first mountain pass. Townes Pass is just over 1500 metres high but the road to the top is 30 kilometres pretty much straight up. I knew I'd be walking for the next few hours as the pass is so steep that only the elite competitors can run up it.

Once the sun went down the temperature dropped to a more bearable 42° Celsius. It still felt bloody hot but at least I didn't feel like my feet were cooking anymore. Even though the temperature was cooler I still needed the crew to keep loading fresh ice into my cap and around my neck. This was probably the one thing that stopped me from going down with heatstroke.

I tried my best to settle back into a good rhythm all the while blocking out the pain of the first serious uphill portion of the race. By this point, I was way ahead of my planned schedule and I took some solace in knowing that the hottest part of the race was over. When I was about three-quarters of the way up Townes Pass, another female runner passed me. She turned as she went past and said, 'See, I told you so'. It was the woman who'd told me I'd gone out too fast earlier in the race. And if that wasn't bad enough, she carried on to say, 'Don't worry it's only a mile to the top of the pass'.

While these might have seemed like encouraging words from a fellow athlete, they turned out to be anything but. It was another

5 miles [8 kilometres] to the top of the pass and she knew it. It still seems pretty weird to me that another runner in such a tough race would bother wasting energy on trying to psych out the other competitors.

I did my best not to let her get to me and focused on walking up the rest of the pass. It was about one in the morning when I made it to the top. The crew were there waiting for me and I decided to take a break. My body had other ideas and soon began shivering like crazy. There was only one thing for it and that was to get back out on the road with a Sustagen in hand. My plan had been to eat like a pig, drink like a fish and run like a tortoise. Two out of three isn't bad — food made me feel nauseous but the electrolyte drinks kept me going.

Sandy joined me to run the 25 kilometres down the other side of Townes Pass. If anyone knew what I was going through at that time it was Sandy. She wasn't named New Zealand ultra-runner of the century in 1999 for nothing. Throughout her career Sandy set five world ultra-running records and once ran a race that was 2000 kilometres long. It was fantastic to have such an amazing role model by my side urging me on.

The combination of having Sandy at my side, the cooler temperature and the downhill run made me feel really strong. The shaking that I'd experienced during my stop at the top of the pass subsided and my energy levels were high, which was a good thing as it was only a few hours before I was staring up to the second pass of the race. In the early morning light, I saw strings of lights rising into the sky. It was a weird sight but I soon realised that it was the headlights of all the support vehicles for runners who were in front of me.

At about 5.30 in the morning, I began passing some of the runners who had started in the two groups before me. While that felt good, the rising sun provided a timely reminder of the hot day that still lay ahead of me.

Panamint Pass was higher than Townes Pass by just over 100 metres but it was a much longer, winding road to the top. The slog to the top felt like it went on forever and by the time I got there the sun was high in the sky and the temperatures had soared back up into the fifties.

Running down the other side of Panamint Pass was a bit easier than running up it, but I suffered from a terrible panic attack when Gerhard told me he didn't think I was going fast enough. In my weakened state, I let that negative thought in for a few minutes and tears started streaming down my face. Eventually, I fought that grain of doubt out of my mind and pulled myself together and refocused on moving forward.

For me, keeping on moving forward is the key to racing. Rather than think about a race in stages or kilometres, I have to break it down into much shorter goals. Sometimes that goal might be the next lamp post, the next energy drink or the next wee break.

By the time I reached the bottom of the pass I'd been running for more than 25 hours and I had another 60 kilometres ahead of me, which I would be running in the heat of the day. The good form I'd felt while running down the previous pass with Sandy had long disappeared. The lack of sleep started to get to me and with it came nausea. It was all I could do to focus on putting one foot in front of the other.

The road stretched out hot and straight ahead of me and I fought with everything in me just to stay awake. I looked up and in the distance I caught a glimpse of Mt Whitney — the finishing point for the race. Appropriately for a desert race, that view of the mountain seemed like a mirage way off in the distance. Even though I could see the end, it was a long way away and, at times, I felt like I'd never reach it.

The real battle in a race like this isn't the physical one — it's the psychological one, the top three inches. Putting one foot in front of the other is one thing. Trying to convince your brain that's what you want to be doing instead of lying down and giving up is where the real fight lies. Somewhere along the straight, my mind just switched off. I remember being aware of Neil running alongside me and talking. Even if I wanted to, I couldn't have answered him. Everything in me was focused on moving forward. My memories of that part of the race are few and far between but Neil will never forget the moment when he accidentally clipped my heel with his foot.

It caused me to trip and fall to the ground. He must have been absolutely mortified but he just kept talking and urging me on. After the fall, the tears came pouring out again and I started to hyperventilate. It took me about 45 minutes to get myself back under control but all the while I kept on moving. There were a few points in the race where I ended up crying. I wasn't too thrilled to be running along bawling my eyes out, but it actually helped to release tension and made me feel better. All the while, little by little, Mt Whitney was coming closer.

Of the next few hours of the race only a couple of things really stick in my mind. At one point, I heard a massive roaring overhead. For a moment I worried that it might have been more thunder bringing more rain. It turned out to be a couple of low-flying jets zooming overhead. The noise of the jets woke me out of myself and

I watched as they flew back and forth across the valley. Suddenly, I felt alive again and I knew that I would make it to the end of the race.

It's pretty amazing how your body can go through ups and downs on a race like this. For a while after I saw the jets, I felt really up. My body had staged a bit of a comeback. But it didn't last. The nausea, the pain and the exhaustion all came crowding back in. That's how it was for most of the race — ups and downs the whole time.

The second thing I remember was Chris bringing me a cell phone. Mum was on the other end of it. Although she's always been my biggest supporter, Mum didn't come to Death Valley with us. She reckons she would have worried too much and I know I would have been worried about her in the heat — it probably wouldn't have helped either of us much.

The sound of Mum's voice back there in New Plymouth was enough to turn on the tears again. I told her I was feeling pretty shattered but that I knew my goal was within my grasp. As always, she encouraged me to go on and reminded me of all the support I had back at home. After I'd talked to Mum, I thought about my project manager, Andrea Needham. Andrea was in hospital having suffered a set-back with her body rejecting her new lungs. It made me realise that my battle would soon be over. Unlike what she had to deal with, my fight to the finish line would be easy. There was no way I was going to give up — too many people, including Andrea, had put too much into me being here for me to quit. I had to keep going.

Hours and kilometres passed in much the same way until the town of Lone Pine came into view. Lone Pine was the site of the final checkpoint for the race and from there all that remained was the punishing climb up Mt Whitney to the finishing point. Arriving at the checkpoint, I was delighted to see Jack Denness again, there to cheer me on. He gave me another big hug and told me he knew I could do it. We both had tears in our eyes — me because I had made it so far and Jack because he knew what was ahead of me.

The final 21 kilometres climbed 2548 metres up the side of the mountain. The gradient for this part of the race was 18 per cent, which is bloody steep. On the up side, I was way ahead of the time I was hoping to do and pretty close to the finish line. The sun set for another day and because Mt Whitney is so much higher above sea level than Death Valley the temperature dropped to a much more bearable 35° Celsius. Even though the end was in sight, the trek up the mountain wasn't without its challenges.

Once I realised I was really going to finish the race I got a bit hysterical. The exhaustion, the nausea and the pain were all taken over by the euphoria that I was actually going to achieve this massive goal I'd set myself. As it was the middle of the night, the crew had lights with them. I was wearing a head mounted torch but Neil was running with me and he had this spotlight. Ahead of me I could see my shadow and in my depleted state, I thought it looked really weird. So I decided it'd be pretty funny to wave my arms around and dance a bit. The crew must have thought I'd flipped when I started pulling out my best Michael Jackson moves! The television crew must have thought they'd struck gold with the potential headline looming 'Ultramarathon Runner Loses Mind Just Short of the Finish Line'.

The elation didn't last long and with only about 5 kilometres to go — the steepest part of the climb — my whole back went into wicked cramps. The pain was excruciating and I kept begging the crew to let me rest for a while. They knew I was in agony but there was no way they were going to let me stop so close to the finish line. I started crying again — I felt like my whole body was bruised and

I didn't know how much more I could take. Fortunately, the doubts didn't have long enough to take hold as the finish line was in my sight within minutes. The crew were all with me to run over the line — it was one of the best moments of my life.

No words can quite explain the elation I felt at that moment. I'd spent so long with this goal in front of me and now I'd achieved it. It was magic. Gerhard, Neil, Sandy and Chris were all there with me and they were the best crew I could have wished for.

When I got my official time, I couldn't believe it — 38 hours, 24 minutes and 43 seconds. Awesome! I'd hoped to do the race in 48 hours and I'd beaten that time by nine and a half hours. I couldn't believe it. I'd averaged 5.65 kilometres an hour and I was the tenth woman home and 22nd overall. It was awesome. I was ecstatic. The race was won by Jorge Pacheco from Mexico. He'd run a time of 23 hours, 20 minutes and 16 seconds. And remember that chick who'd tried to psych me out during the race? I finished nine hours ahead of her.

Hallucinations

Hallucinations are another weird side effect of ultra-running. After I finished Badwater, Chris told me that at one point I was convinced that I was being chased by a bear and another time I thought someone was trying to pee on my shoes. When you're getting low on blood sugars and that sort of thing, your body will do everything to keep you alive and sustain what you're doing. It'll go into survival mode and start doing stuff like drawing minerals out of your bones.

Hallucinations usually start with the fringes of your vision starting to go a bit weird. After that you'll probably start seeing shadows moving. Later still, the ground will start to move. Then the voices and visions might start. There's no way to control them and you have to keep moving through them.

It's important that support people recognise hallucinations for what they are and don't get too emotional about them. When they happen, they should do what they can to support the runner and make sure that they don't hurt themselves.

BURRITOS AND BLISTERS

----

*Develop an attitude of gratitude and acknowledge what others
have given you or contributed to your growth*

Once the elation had subsided a bit, all I could think about was getting
something to eat and having a shower. The desire for food was largely
because I hadn't eaten anything solid for the previous 40 hours. The
combination of extreme temperatures and exhaustion meant that I'd
battled nausea throughout much of the race and I had depended on
drinks for most of my calories. I'd taken in between 8000 and 10,000
calories but I'd expended about 23,000 calories. No wonder I was
hungry!

The first thing I ate after the race was a burrito from a gas station
at about 2 am — that's the American equivalent of getting a pie at
a petrol station in the middle of the night! And you know what, it
actually tasted pretty damn good.

When we got to the motel in Lone Pine, at about 4 am, there was a bit of a problem. I'd finished the race in a much better time than expected and our booking wasn't until the next night. The whole place was booked out. Thankfully, somehow, the guy at reception thought he'd found us a room but when we went up there we spent ages trying the key, to no avail. Then the door opened. We'd been trying the wrong room and had woken up the occupant who was none too happy with us.

Our hopes for a room to ourselves evaporated. In the end the manager let us sleep in the pool area on deck chairs. While the rest of the team were having a few celebratory beers, I managed to get in a shower and examine the damage I'd done to myself. Even though the race was a massive battle, I was in pretty good physical condition at the end. I could stand up OK and, even though I had holes in my back, I didn't have a single blister on my feet! In fact, I'd run the whole race in the same pair of shoes. The time I'd spent getting assessed at Front Runner in New Plymouth had certainly paid off. A lot of runners will go through several pairs of shoes in a race like this. Sometimes, it takes a while to get used to different shoes and that can slow you down. At least I hadn't had to worry about that!

I was in such good form that the day after the race, I left Gerhard, Chris and Neil dealing with their hangovers and went to the local gas station to get the car tyre sorted out! When I got back to the motel they were still carked out but I was feeling pretty good. After a couple of day's recovery, it was time to head home. Gerhard had been such an amazing support for me over the past few days it was really tough to say goodbye to him. But once again, he had to go back to his life in Austria and my life was now firmly ensconced in New Zealand.

Sandy, Neil, Chris and I all turned up at the airport in San

Francisco to check in for our Air New Zealand flight home. Little did we know that Andrea, despite her set-back, had been working her magic from New Plymouth and the Air New Zealand guys were expecting us. We got the full VIP treatment. We were ushered straight to the Koru Lounge and once we were on the flight, one of the crew members made an announcement saying that I was the first New Zealand woman to complete the Badwater Ultramarathon through Death Valley. Everyone was cheering and clapping — it was a great moment. The crew then presented us with a bottle of champagne. It made me realise once again what a great country New Zealand is.

I didn't really need the champagne though — as a result of the fluid retention I'd suffered during the race I ended up weighing 4 kilograms more than when I'd started and I couldn't blame the gas station burrito or the food in the Koru Lounge. Throughout the flight home, I was going to the loo every 20 minutes!

Arriving back in New Plymouth, there was a huge crowd waiting for me at the airport. The reception was amazing. We went straight to Crowded House, a bar in town, where a whole lot of people had paid to have breakfast with me. The jetlag, the pain and the exhaustion I felt were put aside while I celebrated with the people who'd helped me get to Death Valley in the first place. Everyone was so excited for me, including Tim Fowler, a 90-year-old World War II veteran who was so impressed with my achievements that he had come from Waitara to meet me! He was awesome and the reception was fantastic.

The next couple of weeks were really tough for me. While you might think I'd be elated and running round saying 'I did it! I did it!' I was actually physically and mentally shattered. Having achieved the goal I'd focused on for so long, I felt a bit bereft. My body was utterly depleted and even the simplest of daily tasks were a bit challenging for me. I'd lived on adrenaline throughout the race and now my body was depleted of adrenaline and serotonin. That combined with leaving Gerhard again meant that I felt really low. All I wanted to do was climb into bed and stay there for a week while Mum brought me cups of tea!

Over that time I had hundreds of emails and calls from well-wishers. I did heaps of media interviews and the requests for speaking engagements started to flood in. I knew that these were the people who had helped me achieve my goal of running Badwater so there was no way I was going to let them down. I fought the desire to disappear under the duvet and I worked hard to make sure that I thanked all the people who had been so generous to me.

I slowly got back to normal, but it wasn't until I saw the video on *20/20* about a month later that I was able to begin to appreciate what I'd achieved. I watched it with Mum and Dad and it was funny seeing us all on telly. Watching the doco, it really hit me that I'd done it — I'd actually conquered Death Valley.

After the documentary screened, heaps of people started to recognise me whenever I was in Auckland. It was amazing how much that *20/20* show stuck with people. I was used to people in Taranaki knowing who I was, but to get bailed up in a supermarket in Auckland was something else. It was awesome.

The generosity people showed before I went didn't subside after I got back. One day I was sitting in the shop and a guy walked in with a big bunch of flowers and a bottle of champagne. I thought he was probably coming to buy jewellery for his girlfriend to go with the wine and flowers. Mum jokingly said, 'Ohh are they for me? You shouldn't have.' He was really apologetic and said, 'Well, no, they're actually for your daughter.' I couldn't believe it. It turned out he'd come up from Stratford just to congratulate me. How amazing is that?

Even though I felt pretty bad after I got back from Death Valley, I only had four or five days off training before I got back into it. Not long after I got back, I went up to Auckland to do a guest appearance on *Code* on Maori Television. The guys from the show were fantastically supportive of me throughout the whole build-up to Death Valley so it was great to be able to go back and talk to them about my race.

While I was in Auckland I started training with Gerard Fynmore — or Fyn as he's known — at City Fitness in Newmarket. Fyn's an ex-army physical trainer and he really helped me get back from the low that I was in after Death Valley. Setting new goals really helped me to dig myself out of the low — the Auckland Marathon, the 24 Hour Nationals. I managed to run 192.5 kilometres in the 24-hour race at the nationals when my previous best had been 155 kilometres. I was stoked and, when I did that, I knew I was back on track. Maybe, just maybe, I'd run Death Valley again.

December 2008 was an amazing month for me. At the New Zealand Maori Sports Awards in Rotorua I was named Maori Sportswoman of the Year. It was a fantastic night. I attended the ceremony with Mum, Dad, Fyn, Casey, Aunty Peggy and my cousin James. Macca decided he'd come, too, so he ran over from Tauranga! It was a great night and I felt so privileged to even be nominated. Winning was an absolute honour. Being recognised for an award like this was a great pay-off for all the hard work that I'd put in over the years.

That wasn't the last accolade to come my way for the year. At the end of the month, the *Taranaki Daily News* nominated me as their

'Person of the Year'. I couldn't believe it. All I'd ever tried to do was achieve my goals and, at the same time, inspire other people to achieve theirs. Getting this kind of recognition was just a wonderful bonus.

The elation I felt after winning these awards was soon tinged with sadness. In early January, Andrea Needham, my dynamic project manager, passed away. Without Andrea's unbelievable energy and support, I don't know if I would have made it to Death Valley. She was such an inspiration to me. Her strength and determination to fight her illness was an inspiration to me. And I know she would have been proud of me for setting some new goals — one of which was to run Badwater again in 2009.

That's right. I decided to go back and run Death Valley again. I believe I've got a few more years left in me at this caper and I'm going to make the most of them. The older I get the more experienced I am and the more tricks I know. But on the flipside of that I also have to stay fitter and work harder than when I was younger. The body is an amazing thing and it does recover from terrible hardships. When I give mine a little bit of time and a little bit of space it comes back stronger than ever. Ageing slows everything down, but at the moment I'm the strongest I've ever been. I'm still doing personal bests and I've got to know my body and how much it can handle more than I have before.

POSTSCRIPT

I made it! I finished Badwater 2009 with a time of 37 hours and 14 minutes. I beat my time from last year by an hour. I was the eighth woman home, which was two places ahead of last year. I'm absolutely stoked.

Once again, I had an amazing crew with me so a huge thank you to Megan Stewart, Jaron Mumby, Chris Cruikshank, Casey Potatau, Murray Dick and Howard Dell.

I'd also like to thank my amazing sponsors: Taranaki Engineering, Taranaki Steelform, Bartercard, Mobilize, Buff Head Gear and Fire Design. Thanks also to my clothing and footwear sponsor adidas, Will Hinchcliff at EECP and More FM.

ACKNOWLEDGEMENTS

There's no way I could do what I do without the support of a whole
lot of people. I'd like to thank everyone who has had a part in getting
me to where I am today — without you I wouldn't be able to run.

The following people have all helped me in numerous ways, so
thanks to: Inge and Marcel Vercammen from Van Dyck's; Murray
and Jane Dick from Taranaki Engineering; Darrell Back from Taranaki
Steelformers; Paul Bolte and Stuart Wilkinson from Bartercard; Marco
Streibel from Buff Headwear; Kerry and Sarah Hamilton; the More
FM crew — Anne Meyer, Renata Hayward, Mark Jamieson, Beth and
Waggs and rest of the team; Frontrunner New Plymouth — Kelvin
and Michelle Giddy, Paul Ballinger; Neale and Fiona Parkinson and
Richard Valentine at Bayleys Real Estate; Red 8 — Jim and Robena
Bedwell; Malcolm Stobie and the Thompson's Nutrition team; Bruce
from Adviso Ltd; Kendall North Nutrition; Lauren Hann from Hanns
On massage; Fire Design; David Casey and Angela Koot from Big

Media; Will Hinchcliff and the team at EECP Primary Heart Care; Angus Campbell; Megan, John and Cameron Stewart at Mobilize; City Fitness, especially Neil and Sam Wagstaff; Mayor Peter and Rosemary Tennent; Howie Tamati; Gordon Brown; Bruce Richards; Ross Fanthorpe and the team from Govett Quilliam lawyers; Bridget Burke; all my fashion show models; Greg 'Mr Pumpkin' Edley; Glenn Edley and Spikemail; Shane Cameron; Phil and Elsa Kingsley Jones; Eileen Tamati; all the Biz at Home ladies; Alex Mckenzie; John and Val Muskett; Mike Scott; Rob Tucker; Cameron Brewer and the Newmarket Business Association; adidas especially Kayne Henderson; Nic McCloy my wonderful author; Abba Renshaw and the whole Allen and Unwin team; Hemi Takarua; Glen Osborne; Debbie Longhurst; Don and Leonie Crow; Irena Brooks; Murray Chong and Karen Upson; Sandwich Extreme; TK and Piri Wano; Whare and Emma Wano; Peter Tainui; Liam Courtenay; Sam Scannell; Dr Andrew Kilding; Kelly Sheerin; Sharon Jones; and Stars Travel.

A big thank you to my wonderful Death Valley crewmembers Megan Stewart, Sandy Barwick, Neil Wagstaff, Chris Cruikshank, Gerhard Lusskandl, Howard Dell, Casey Potatau and Jaron Mumby;

To my dearly loved family: Mum Isobel, Dad Cyril, Dawson, Mitchell, Aunty Peggy, James, Kim and Victoria. Thank you for being their through the good and the bad times, for your stability, your love, your dedication, your tolerance and understanding. For believing in me and helping me up when I stumbled. I will love you all forever.

Mum you have given up your life for us kids you are the most precious person in the world. Dad you loved us with all your heart, and fought for us always, sacrificing much on the way. Thank you.

To Gerhard: you are part of my soul and I will carry you forever in my heart. Thank you for everything.